A Taste of Brunch

by Jacquie Schmit ❧ Eileen Mandryk ❧ Jo Wuth

Three Sisters Publishing Inc.

Front Cover Photograph
Blueberries and Cream French Toast, page 24
Blueberry Orange Sauce, page 24,

A TASTE OF BRUNCH
by
Jacquie Schmit ⸺ Eileen Mandryk ⸺ Jo Wuth

First Printing – August 1999

Copyright © 1999 by
Three Sisters Publishing Inc.
12234 – 49 Street
Edmonton, Alberta
Canada T5W 3A8
www.3sistersbooks.com

CANADIAN CATALOGUING IN PUBLICATION DATA
Schmit, Jacquie
    A taste of brunch
    Includes index.
    ISBN 1-894022-33-5

1. Brunches.   I. Mandryk, Eileen
II. Wuth, Jo   III. Title.

TX733.S39 1999   641.5'3   C99-920124-7

Photography by:
Merle Prosofsky, Merle Prosofsky Photography, Edmonton, Alberta

Dishes, Accessories and Flowers courtesy of:
Call the Kettle Black
Kuhlmann's Market Garden & Greenhouses Ltd.
Libicz's Kitchen Essentials
Stokes

Page Formatting and Index by Iona Glabus

Designed, Printed and Produced in Canada by:
Centax Books, a Division of Publishing Solutions/PW Group
Publishing Director, Photo Designer & Food Stylist: Margo Embury
1150 Eighth Avenue, Regina, Saskatchewan, Canada S4R 1C9
(306) 525-2304   FAX (306) 757-2439
E-mail: centax@printwest.com   www.centaxbooks.com

Table of Contents

Recipes have been tested in U.S. Standard measurements. Common metric measurements are given as a convenience for those who are more familiar with metric. Recipes have not been tested in metric.

Introduction

We somehow take for granted
The things that are most important to us
Good friends, loving family and all nature that surrounds us
Let's thank God for all our blessings

In our fast and busy pace of life
We need to stop along the way
To drink in God's artistry we pass by every day
Let's thank God for all our blessings

Take time to smell the new-mown grass
The laughter of children at play
The music of God's creatures; listen to what they say
Let's thank God for all our blessings

Enjoy our majestic snow-capped peaks
Our green forests, that abound with game
Our grain fields in the golden sun that have brought
                                    our farmers fame
Let's thank God for all our blessings.

by Jo Wuth for the Sisters three

We were born and raised the Campbell girls in the farming community of Lamont, Alberta. Our first book *A Taste of Christmas* reflects the special magical times of our family Christmas traditions. We hope that you will enjoy this new collection – our favorite brunch recipes to share with your family and friends all year long.

Griddle & Baked Cakes

Pancakes

Crêpes

Waffles

French Toast

Fluffy Buttermilk Pancakes

1¾ cups	flour	425 mL
2 tbsp.	sugar	30 mL
1½ tsp.	baking soda	7 mL
1 tsp.	cream of tartar	5 mL
½ tsp.	salt	2 mL
2 cups	buttermilk	500 mL
4	eggs, separated	4
¼ cup	butter OR margarine, melted OR vegetable oil	60 mL

In a large bowl combine flour, sugar, baking soda, cream of tartar and salt. Stir well to combine. In another large bowl, whisk together buttermilk and egg yolks. Beat flour mixture into buttermilk mixture along with the melted butter or margarine. In a small bowl, beat egg whites until stiff and fold into pancake batter.

Heat a large skillet over medium-high heat. Lightly brush with vegetable oil. In batches, ladle in scant ⅓ cup (75 mL) batter for each pancake; cook until set and bubbly on top, about 2 minutes. Flip pancakes; cook 1 minute, until cooked through. Serve immediately.

Makes 20, 4" (10 cm) pancakes

Blueberry Pancakes

Remember those famous childhood treats, big fresh blueberry pancakes.

2 cups	flour	500 mL
1 tsp.	baking soda	5 mL
1 tsp.	salt	5 mL
2 tbsp.	sugar	30 mL
2	eggs, slightly beaten	2
2 cups	buttermilk	500 mL
2 tbsp.	vegetable oil	30 mL
1 cup	blueberries, fresh or frozen (if using frozen, thaw and drain)	250 mL

Blueberry Pancakes *(continued)*

In a large bowl, combine flour, baking soda, salt and sugar. In another bowl, beat eggs slightly; add buttermilk and vegetable oil; stir into the flour mixture, stirring only until mixture is moistened. Gently fold in blueberries. Bake on a medium hot, lightly greased griddle or skillet. Turn pancakes when surface bubbles break and edges are turning dry; cook about 1 minute. Serve immediately. Top with fresh butter and maple syrup.

Makes 10-12 pancakes

Blueberry Pancake and Waffle Syrup

A nice fresh fruit flavor.

2 cups	blueberries, fresh or frozen (thawed)	500 mL
⅓ cup	sugar	75 mL
⅓ cup	water	75 mL
½ tsp.	ground nutmeg	2 mL
½ tsp.	vanilla	2 mL

In a small saucepan, combine blueberries, sugar, water and nutmeg. Place over medium heat and bring to a boil. Reduce heat to low; simmer for 8-10 minutes, or until syrup is thickened. Remove from heat and stir in vanilla. Serve immediately or refrigerate to use at another time.

Makes 1½ cups (375 mL)

Sunshine Pancakes

Oatmeal and orange juice all in one dish.

1 cup	EACH, quick-cooking oats, flour	250 mL
2 tbsp.	sugar	30 mL
2 tsp.	baking powder	10 mL
1 tsp.	salt	5 mL
2 tbsp.	grated orange rind	30 mL
2	eggs, lightly beaten	2
1 cup	milk	250 mL
½ cup	orange juice	125 mL
¼ cup	vegetable oil	60 mL

In a large bowl, combine oats, flour, sugar, baking powder, salt and orange rind. Make a well in the center. In another bowl, beat eggs lightly and add milk, orange juice and oil; pour into well and stir just until moistened. Pour batter by ¼ cupfuls (60 mL) onto a lightly greased hot griddle; turn when bubbles form on top of pancakes. Cook until second side is golden brown. Serve immediately.

Serves 6

Maple Apple Topping

⅔ cup	maple syrup	150 mL
½ cup	orange juice	125 mL
¼ cup	brown sugar	60 mL
2 tbsp.	butter OR margarine	30 mL
5	apples, peeled, cored, thinly sliced	5
⅓ cup	raisins, washed, dried	75 mL
1 tbsp.	cornstarch	15 mL
1 tbsp.	cold water	15 mL

In a skillet, whisk syrup, juice and sugar; bring to boil over medium heat. Add butter; boil for 1 minute. Add apples and raisins; cover; cook for 5 minutes, until apples are tender; stir occasionally. Dissolve cornstarch in cold water; add to apples; cook and stir for 1 minute, until thickened. Serve warm over pancakes, French toast or waffles.

Apple Nut Pancakes with Apple Syrup

1 cup	flour	250 mL
2 tbsp.	sugar	30 mL
2 tsp.	baking powder	10 mL
½ tsp.	salt	2 mL
½ tsp.	ground cinnamon	2 mL
¾ cup	milk	175 mL
3 tbsp.	butter OR margarine, melted	45 mL
2 tsp.	vanilla	10 mL
2	egg whites	2
½ cup	apples, peeled, shredded, or finely chopped	125 mL
½ cup	chopped walnuts	125 mL

In a large bowl, combine flour, sugar, baking powder, salt and cinnamon. In another bowl, combine milk, butter and vanilla; mix well and stir into the dry ingredients, just until combined. Beat egg whites until stiff peaks form; fold into batter along with apple and nuts. Pour batter by ¼ cupfuls (60 mL) onto a lightly greased hot griddle; turn when bubbles form on top. Cook until second side is golden brown.

Makes 10-12 pancakes

Apple Syrup

¼ cup	sugar	60 mL
4 tsp.	cornstarch	20 mL
¼ tsp.	ground allspice	1 mL
1½ cups	apple juice	375 mL

Combine sugar, cornstarch and allspice in a medium saucepan; stir in apple juice. Cook and stir over medium heat until thickened, about 6-8 minutes. Serve over pancakes.

Makes about 1½ cups (375 mL) of syrup

Baked Strawberry Pancake

A delicious puffed pancake filled with strawberries and whipped cream. Any fresh fruit may be substituted for the strawberries.

4 cups	sliced strawberries, fresh or frozen, (thawed, drained)	1 L
2 tbsp.	sugar	30 mL
2 tsp.	lemon juice	10 mL
3	eggs	3
½ cup	flour	125 mL
½ cup	milk	125 mL
½ tsp.	salt	2 mL
2 tbsp.	butter OR margarine	30 mL
	whipped cream OR sour cream, (optional)	

Preheat oven to 400°F (200°C). Combine strawberries with sugar and lemon juice; set aside. In a bowl, beat eggs until fluffy. Add flour, milk and salt; beat until smooth. Place butter in a 10" (25 cm) skillet; heat in oven for 3-5 minutes. Immediately pour batter into hot skillet. Bake for 25-30 minutes, until pancake has risen and is puffed all over. Remove from oven and fill with sliced strawberries. Cut into wedges; serve immediately with whipped cream or sour cream if desired.

Serves 4-6

Strawberry Syrup

2 cups	strawberries, fresh or frozen (thawed), mashed	500 mL
⅓ cup	sugar	75 mL
⅓ cup	water	75 mL
1 tsp.	lemon juice	5 mL

In a small saucepan, combine strawberries, sugar and water. Place over medium heat and bring to a boil. Reduce heat to low; simmer for 8-10 minutes, or until syrup is thickened. Remove from heat and stir in lemon juice. Serve immediately or refrigerate to use at another time.

Makes 1½ cups (375 mL)

Cheddar Mushroom Puff Pancake

2 tbsp.	butter OR margarine	30 mL
3	eggs	3
1¼ cups	milk	300 mL
¾ cup	flour	175 mL
2 tbsp.	butter OR margarine	30 mL
1 lb.	fresh mushrooms, sliced	500 g
3	green onions, chopped	3
2 tbsp.	white wine	30 mL
⅓ cup	sour cream	75 mL
1 tbsp.	flour	15 mL
¼ tsp.	salt	1 mL
¼ tsp.	pepper	1 mL
1 cup	shredded Cheddar cheese	250 mL

Preheat oven to 375°F (190°C). Place 2 tbsp. (30 mL) butter in a 2-quart (2 L) round, shallow baking dish. While oven preheats, set dish in oven until butter melts and is hot. In a large bowl, beat eggs 1-2 minutes; gradually add milk; combine well. Add flour and continue beating for 1-2 minutes. Pour batter into hot butter and bake for 30-45 minutes, or until puffed and golden. While pancake is baking, prepare sauce. In a large skillet over medium-high heat, melt 2 tbsp. (30 mL) butter; add mushrooms and onions and cook until lightly browned, about 3 minutes. Pour in wine; cover and cook for additional 2 minutes. In a small bowl, blend sour cream with flour, salt and pepper. Stir into mushrooms and cook, stirring until blended and mixture begins to boil. Sprinkle in shredded Cheddar cheese. Remove from heat and cover mixture. When pancake is baked; cut into wedges; top with cheese mushroom mixture and serve immediately.

Serves 4-6

Pancakes with Bacon

Yummy! The bacon is cooked right in the pancake – serve with maple syrup.

20	bacon strips	20
2 cups	flour	500 mL
½ tsp.	salt	2 mL
2	eggs	2
3 cups	milk	750 mL

In a large skillet over medium-high heat, cook bacon until browned and crisp, approximately 10 minutes. Drain bacon on paper towels; carefully pour off bacon drippings and reserve. In a large bowl combine flour and salt. In another bowl, beat eggs and milk together. Gradually add egg mixture to the flour mixture, whisking constantly to avoid any lumps.

In a skillet, over medium heat, place 2 strips of the cooked bacon and ½ tsp. (2 mL) of the reserved bacon drippings. Using ½ cup (125 mL) of batter for each pancake, pour batter into skillet, tilting pan so batter flows evenly to edges. Cook pancake 1-2 minutes, or until bottom is set and slightly golden. Turn pancake and cook for additional 1-2 minutes, or until lightly browned. Continue cooking as above until all bacon and batter is used. Stack pancakes between sheets of waxed paper on baking sheet and keep warm in 225°F (107°C) oven or serve immediately with maple syrup.

Makes 10 pancakes

Brown Sugar Syrup

Mom made this recipe all the time when she served pancakes.

2 cups	brown sugar	500 mL
1 cup	water	250 mL
1 tsp.	vanilla	5 mL

Brown Sugar Syrup *(continued)*

In a medium saucepan, combine sugar and water. Place over medium heat and bring to a boil, stirring constantly to dissolve sugar. Lower heat; boil gently about 15 minutes, or until syrupy. Remove from heat and stir in vanilla.

Makes 1⅔ cups (400 mL)

Variation:

 For *Maple Syrup*, use 1-2 tsp. (5-10 mL) of maple flavoring instead of vanilla.

Corn Pancakes

These are great served with maple syrup; the corn adds flavor and texture.

1 cup	flour	250 mL
½ cup	cornmeal	125 mL
1 tbsp.	sugar	15 mL
½ tsp.	baking soda	2 mL
½ tsp.	salt	2 mL
2 cups	buttermilk	500 mL
¾ cup	cooked corn kernels	175 mL
2 tbsp.	vegetable oil	30 mL

In a large bowl, combine flour, cornmeal, sugar, baking soda and salt. In a small bowl, stir together buttermilk, corn and vegetable oil. Make a well in the center of the flour mixture; add buttermilk mixture to flour mixture and stir well to combine. Heat skillet over medium-high heat; brush lightly with vegetable oil. Working in batches, ladle a scant ¼ cup (60 mL) batter for each pancake. Cook until set and bubbly on top, about 2 minutes. Turn pancakes over; cook another 1-2 minutes, until cooked through. Stack between sheets of waxed paper and keep warm in 225°F (107°C) oven or serve immediately. Serve with bacon or ham and maple syrup.

Makes 18, 4" (10 cm) pancakes

Spinach Pancakes

These may seem unusual, but they are delicious served with grated old Cheddar cheese or a cheese sauce.

10 oz.	pkg. frozen chopped spinach (thawed)	283 g
¾ cup	milk	175 mL
¼ cup	chopped parsley	60 mL
3	green onions, chopped	3
3	eggs	3
½ cup	half-and-half cereal cream	125 mL
¼ cup	mayonnaise	60 mL
1 tbsp.	melted butter	15 mL
¾ cup	flour	175 mL
¼ tsp.	salt	1 mL
⅛ tsp.	pepper	0.5 mL
	vegetable oil for frying	

Drain and squeeze moisture from chopped spinach. In a large skillet combine the spinach and milk. Stir well to combine. Place over low heat and slowly bring to a boil. Stir in parsley and green onions. Cover and remove from heat. In a large bowl, lightly beat eggs; add half and half cereal cream, mayonnaise and melted butter; mix well. Stir in flour, salt and pepper, then add a few tablespoons of the spinach mixture. Add remaining spinach mixture and stir well. Set aside for 15 minutes. Brush a large skillet with oil, heat over medium heat. Pour in approximately 2 tbsp. (30 mL) of the spinach mixture for each pancake; cook for 2 minutes, or until edges are browned; turn and cook for 2 more minutes. Remove to serving plate and serve immediately.

Makes 10-12 pancakes

Basic Crêpes

2	eggs	2
2 cups	flour	500 mL
1 tsp.	salt	5 mL
1 tsp.	sugar	5 mL
1¾-2 cups	milk	425-500 mL

In a large bowl, beat eggs lightly. Combine flour, salt and sugar; add to eggs. Beat in enough milk to make a thin batter. Lightly grease crêpe pan or 6-7" (15-18 cm) skillet and heat over medium-high heat. Pour in about 2 tbsp. (30 mL) of batter. Fry crêpes on both sides and roll up immediately. Continue until all batter is used. Cover crêpes and set aside while preparing filling.

Makes 15-20 crêpes

Bacon 'n' Egg Crêpes

Bacon and eggs served in a crêpe. Top with Hollandaise Sauce, page 97.

1 lb.	bacon, cooked and crumbled	500 g
8	eggs	8
¼ cup	whipping cream	60 mL
¼ cup	chopped green onion	60 mL
¼ tsp.	salt	1 mL
⅛ tsp.	pepper	0.5 mL
1 cup	shredded Cheddar cheese	250 mL
8	large crêpes	8

In a skillet over medium-high heat, cook bacon until crisp; drain; crumble and set aside. In a large bowl, whisk together eggs and cream. Stir in bacon, onions and seasonings. Over medium heat, in a large skillet, cook egg mixture. As portions cook, gently lift with a spatula so that uncooked portions can flow underneath. Avoid constant stirring. Sprinkle cheese over eggs when eggs are almost totally cooked. Spoon egg mixture into crêpes and roll up. Serve immediately.

Serves 8

Banana Crêpes

A luxurious, rich, brunch treat.

Crêpes:

1 cup	flour	250 mL
¼ cup	icing (confectioner's) sugar	60 mL
1 cup	milk	250 mL
2	eggs	2
3 tbsp.	butter OR margarine, melted	45 mL
1 tsp.	vanilla	5 mL
¼ tsp.	salt	1 mL

Banana Cinnamon Filling:

¼ cup	butter OR margarine	60 mL
¼ cup	brown sugar	60 mL
1 tsp.	ground cinnamon	5 mL
¼ cup	half-and-half cereal cream	60 mL
6	bananas, halved lengthwise	6
	whipped cream and additional cinnamon (optional)	

Crêpes: In a large bowl, combine flour and icing sugar. Add milk, eggs, butter, vanilla and salt; beat until smooth. Heat a lightly greased 6" (15 cm) skillet; add about 3 tbsp. (45 mL) of batter, spreading to almost cover bottom of skillet. Fry crêpes on both sides and roll up immediately. Repeat with remaining batter; greasing skillet as needed.

Filling: Melt butter in a large skillet. Stir in brown sugar and cinnamon. Stir in cream and cook until slightly thickened. Add half of the bananas at a time to skillet; heat for 2-3 minutes, spooning sauce over them. Remove from the heat. Roll a crêpe around each banana half and place on a serving plate. Spoon sauce over pancakes. Top with whipped cream and a dash of cinnamon if desired.

Serves 5-6

Bridal Shower Brunch

White Sangria, page 158

Chilled Raspberry Soup, page 78*

Savory Crab Cheesecake, page 111

Strawberry and Cheese Salad, page 60*

Layered Chicken Salad, page 67

Eileen's Tea Biscuits, page 32

Herbed Scones, page 31*

Dream Cake, page 150

Strawberry Fancies, page 142

Chocolate-Dipped Strawberries, page 141

* Pictured recipes

Chilled Raspberry Soup
Strawberry and Cheese Salad
Herbed Scones

Orange Spiced Whole-Wheat Waffles

1½ cups	whole-wheat flour	375 mL
½ cup	all-purpose flour	125 mL
¼ cup	EACH, wheat germ, unprocessed bran	60 mL
4 tsp.	baking powder	20 mL
1 tsp.	baking soda	5 mL
½ tsp.	ground nutmeg	2 mL
½ tsp.	salt	2 mL
2	eggs	2
2 cups	buttermilk	500 mL
½ cup	orange juice	125 mL
¼ cup	vegetable oil	60 mL
¼ cup	packed brown sugar	60 mL
2 tsp.	grated orange rind	10 mL

Coat waffle iron with nonstick spray and preheat. In a large bowl, combine flours, wheat germ, bran, baking powder, baking soda, nutmeg and salt; set aside. In a medium bowl, beat eggs lightly; stir in buttermilk, juice, oil, sugar and orange rind. Add the liquid ingredients to the dry, mixing just enough to moisten completely. Bake in preheated waffle iron, 3-5 minutes, until crisp and brown. Serve hot with butter and syrup or your favorite topping.

Makes 6-8 waffles

Banana Maple Sauce

2 tbsp.	butter	30 mL
4	bananas, sliced	4
1⅔ cups	Brown Sugar Syrup, page 12 OR regular pancake syrup	400 mL
1 tsp.	maple flavoring	5 mL
½ tsp.	vanilla	2 mL

In a large skillet, over medium heat, melt butter; add sliced bananas. Cook, stirring constantly for approximately 3 minutes. Pour syrup over bananas; stir in maple and vanilla flavorings; cook for additional 3-4 minutes. Serve warm over pancakes, waffles or French toast.

Serves 4-6

Chocolate Delight Waffles

A chocolate waffle with chocolate syrup – a chocolate lover's delight.

2 cups	flour	500 mL
½ cup	unsweetened cocoa powder	125 mL
1 tsp.	baking soda	5 mL
½ tsp.	salt	2 mL
½ cup	butter OR margarine, softened	125 mL
¾ cup	sugar	175 mL
2	eggs	2
1 tsp.	vanilla	5 mL
2 cups	buttermilk	500 mL
3 cups	vanilla ice cream	750 mL

In a large bowl, combine flour, cocoa, baking soda and salt. In another large bowl, beat butter and sugar until smooth and creamy. Beat in eggs, 1 at a time; add vanilla. Beat in flour mixture, alternately with buttermilk; beginning and ending with flour mixture.

Make waffles in waffle maker following manufacturer's directions. Keep warm in oven until ready to serve. Serve waffles with ice cream and top with about 2 tbsp. (30 mL) of Chocolate Mocha Syrup.

Makes 20, 4" (10 cm) waffles

Chocolate Mocha Syrup

8 x 1 oz.	squares semisweet OR bittersweet chocolate, chopped	8 x 30 g
½ cup	whipping cream	125 mL
¼ cup	brewed strong black coffee	60 mL

In a heavy saucepan, over low heat, combine the chopped chocolate, cream and coffee. Heat, stirring constantly, until the chocolate is completely melted and mixture is smooth.

French Toast Deluxe

Fresh Fruit Salad:

¼ cup	fresh strawberries, sliced	60 mL
¼ cup	green grapes, halved	60 mL
¼ cup	cantaloupe, diced	60 mL
¼ cup	honeydew melon, diced	60 mL

French Toast:

4	eggs	4
½ cup	milk	125 mL
¼ tsp.	salt	1 mL
¼ tsp.	cinnamon	1 mL
8	slices French bread, sliced ½" (1.3 cm)	8
	oil OR butter for frying	
4	eggs	4
4	slices ham, thickly sliced	4
	icing (confectioner's) sugar for garnish	

Fruit Salad: In a small bowl, combine all fruit and set aside.

French Toast: In a large bowl, beat the eggs slightly; add milk, salt and cinnamon. Beat together until well blended. Transfer mixture to a shallow bowl or dish. Dip bread into egg mixture 1 slice at a time. Drain bread slightly and brown in a heated skillet over medium-high heat. Turn and fry second side until golden brown. Remove from pan; set aside and keep warm. In a skillet, over medium heat, fry eggs and ham.

To Assemble: Place 1 slice of French toast on each of 4 serving plates; top each with 1 slice of ham; 1 fried egg; and another slice of French toast (like a sandwich). Place ¼ of the fruit salad on top of each and sprinkle with icing sugar. Serve immediately.

Serves 4

Peaches and Cream Breakfast

Scrumptious – top with maple syrup, cream or ice cream.

12	slices white bread OR egg bread	12
8 oz.	cream cheese, cubed	250 g
2 cups	sliced fresh or canned peaches	500 mL
10	eggs	10
2 cups	milk	500 mL
½ cup	maple syrup	125 mL
1 tsp.	ground cinnamon	5 mL

Remove and discard crusts from bread; cut bread into cubes. Toss lightly with cream cheese cubes. Place half the bread mixture in a greased 9 x 13" (23 x 33 cm) baking pan; layer peach slices over the bread mixture and top with the remaining bread mixture. In a large mixing bowl, beat eggs. Add milk, syrup and cinnamon; mix well. Pour over bread mixture. Cover and refrigerate 8 hours or overnight. Remove from refrigerator 30 minutes before baking. Bake at 375°F (190°C), uncovered, 40-45 minutes, until a knife inserted near center comes out clean. Let stand 5 minutes before cutting.

Serves 6-8

Overnight Apple French Toast

The classic flavors of apple and cinnamon in a sophisticated overnight dish.

1 cup	brown sugar	250 mL
½ cup	butter OR margarine	125 mL
2 tbsp.	light corn syrup	30 mL
2	large apples, peeled, ¼" (1 cm) slices	2
2 tsp.	ground cinnamon	10 mL
3	eggs	3
1 cup	milk	250 mL
1 tsp.	vanilla	5 mL
9	slices day-old French bread, sliced ¾" (2 cm) thick	9

Overnight Apple French Toast *(continued)*

In a small saucepan, cook brown sugar, butter and syrup until thick, 5-7 minutes. Pour into an ungreased 9 x 13" (23 x 33 cm) pan; arrange apples on top; sprinkle with cinnamon. In a mixing bowl, beat eggs, milk and vanilla. Dip bread slices into the egg mixture and place over apples. Cover and refrigerate overnight. Remove from the refrigerator 30 minutes before baking. Bake at 350°F (180°C), uncovered, for 35-40 minutes, or until a knife comes out clean. Let stand 5 minutes.

Serves 4-5

Overnight Oven French Toast

A classic French toast make-ahead with cinnamon, nutmeg and mace.

1	loaf of bread, cut into 1" (2.5 cm) slices	1
12	eggs	12
3 cups	milk	750 mL
¼ tsp.	salt	1 mL
2 tbsp.	sugar	30 mL
1 tsp.	vanilla	5 mL
1 tbsp.	sugar	15 mL
2 tsp.	cinnamon	10 mL
½ tsp.	EACH, ground nutmeg, mace	2 mL
3 tbsp.	butter OR margarine	45 mL

Arrange bread slices in a greased 9 x 13" (23 x 33 cm) baking dish, overlapping slightly. In a medium bowl, whisk eggs, milk, 2 tbsp. (30 mL) sugar, salt and vanilla. Pour slowly over bread slices. Spoon any egg mixture not absorbed by bread back over bread slices, lifting individual slices as needed. In a small bowl, combine sugar, cinnamon, nutmeg and mace. Sprinkle evenly over bread. Dot with butter. Cover and refrigerate overnight.

To bake, remove from refrigerator and uncover, place in oven and bake at 325°F (160°C) for 40-45 minutes, until knife comes out clean. Serve immediately with any syrup or fruit sauces.

Serves 8

Blueberries and Cream French Toast

A delightful way to enjoy your blueberries and cream.

8 oz.	cream cheese, softened	250 g
⅓ cup	sugar	75 mL
1 tsp.	vanilla	5 mL
¼ cup	butter OR margarine, softened	60 mL
1	orange, grated rind of	1
4	eggs	4
1½ cups	milk	375 mL
1	loaf of French bread, cut into 1" (2.5 cm) slices	1
1-2 cups	blueberries, fresh or frozen (thawed)	250-500 mL

In a large bowl, combine cream cheese, sugar, vanilla, butter and orange rind. Add eggs 1 at a time, mixing well after each addition. Stir in milk. Arrange bread slices in rows, slightly overlapping each other, in a greased 9 x 13" (23 x 33 cm) baking dish. Pour cream cheese mixture evenly over bread. Cover with plastic wrap; let stand 15-30 minutes. Just before baking, uncover; sprinkle blueberries on top. Bake at 325°F (160°C) for 45-60 minutes, until golden brown. Serve warm with Blueberry Orange Sauce.

Serves 6-8

Blueberry Orange Sauce

½ cup	sugar	125 mL
1 tbsp.	cornstarch	15 mL
1 cup	water	250 mL
1	orange, grated rind and juice of	1
1 cup	blueberries, fresh or frozen (thawed)	250 mL

In a medium-sized saucepan combine sugar and cornstarch; blend in water, orange rind and juice and blueberries. Over medium heat, stir ring constantly, cook until mixture is thickened and clear. Serve warm.

Both recipes pictured on the front cover.

Quick & Yeast Breads

Doughnuts
Biscuits
Scones
Muffins
Coffeecakes
Sweet Buns

Aunt Susie's Drop Doughnuts

One of our favorite aunts made these spicy little cake doughnuts for us.

2 cups	sugar	500 mL
2 cups	milk	500 mL
2 tsp.	salt	10 mL
2 tsp.	ground nutmeg	10 mL
6	egg yolks, beaten	6
6 cups	flour	1.5 L
5 tbsp.	vegetable oil OR melted shortening	75 mL
6 tsp.	baking powder	30 mL
6	egg whites, well-beaten	6
	vegetable oil for frying	
	sugar OR icing (confectioner's) sugar to coat	

In a large bowl, combine sugar, milk, salt and nutmeg. Stir until sugar is dissolved. Add the beaten egg yolks; combine well. Stir in 5 cups (1.25 L) of flour; set aside the sixth cup of flour. Add the oil; beat well. Combine baking powder with the remaining cup of flour; add to mixture; beat well. Fold in beaten egg whites. Drop batter by teaspoonfuls (5 mL) into hot oil (375°F [190°C]). Fry 2-3 minutes, until golden brown. Remove from oil; drain on paper towels. If desired, while doughnuts are warm, roll in sugar or icing sugar to coat. These freeze well.

Makes 75-80 doughnuts

Apple Fritters

1½ cups	flour	375 mL
2½ tsp.	baking powder	12 mL
1 tsp.	salt	5 mL
2 tbsp.	sugar	30 mL
1 tsp.	ground nutmeg	5 mL
2	eggs	2
½ cup	milk	125 mL
2 cups	apples, peeled, cored, chopped	500 mL

Apple Fritters *(continued)*

In a large bowl, combine flour, baking powder, salt, sugar and nutmeg. In another bowl, lightly beat the eggs; add milk and apples. Make a well in the flour mixture and add the egg mixture; stir until well combined. Drop batter by level tablespoonfuls (15 mL) into hot oil (375°F [190°C]). Fry 2-3 minutes, until golden brown. Remove from hot oil and drain on paper towel. Fritters can be sprinkled with icing (confectioner's) sugar or dipped into a glaze.

Makes 36 fritters

Welsh Cakes

This recipe is from a dear friend, Doreen – it has been in the Roberts family for generations.

3 cups	flour	750 mL
3 tsp.	baking powder	15 mL
1 tsp.	salt	5 mL
1 cup	sugar	250 mL
1 tsp.	ground cinnamon OR nutmeg	5 mL
1 cup	butter OR margarine	250 mL
1 cup	raisins OR currents, washed, dried	250 mL
½ cup	mixed peel	125 mL
2	eggs, lightly beaten	2
½ cup	milk	125 mL

In a large bowl, combine flour, baking powder, salt, sugar and cinnamon. Cut in the butter with pastry blender or 2 knives until crumbly. Add the raisins and mixed peel. In a small bowl, whisk eggs lightly; add milk and combine well. Stir egg mixture into the flour mixture and combine well. Turn dough out onto a lightly floured surface; roll dough out to approximately ½" (1.3 cm) thick. Cut into rounds with cookie cutter. Heat electric frying pan to 325°F (160°C), or cook in a skillet over medium heat 10-12 minutes on each side. Cool on a wire rack. Serve immediately or wrap well and freeze for up to 3 months.

Makes 24 cakes

English Tea Scones

2 cups	flour	500 mL
1 tsp.	baking powder	5 mL
½ tsp.	salt	2 mL
½ cup	butter OR margarine, softened	125 mL
⅓ cup	sugar	75 mL
1	egg, lightly beaten	1
¾ cup	milk	175 mL
1	egg, lightly beaten	1
	sugar	

Preheat oven to 425°F (220°C). In a large bowl, combine flour, baking powder and salt. Cut in butter with a pastry blender or 2 knives. Add sugar and mix lightly. Add 1 egg and milk; stir to make a soft dough. Turn dough out onto a lightly floured pastry board; roll out into an 8" (20 cm) circle. Place dough on a lightly greased cookie sheet. Cut into 8 wedges. Brush with second lightly beaten egg and sprinkle with sugar. Bake for 15-20 minutes, or until golden brown. Serve warm from the oven with butter and jam or preserves.

Makes 8 scones

Variations:

Ginger Walnut Scones: Add ¼ cup (60 mL) chopped crystallized ginger and ¼ cup (60 mL) chopped walnuts to the ⅓ cup (75 mL) of sugar in the above recipe.

Orange Pecan Scones: Add ¼ cup (60 mL) chopped pecans to the ⅓ cup (75 mL) sugar in the above recipe. Sprinkle scones with a mixture of ¼ cup (60 mL) sugar and 1 tbsp. (15 mL) grated orange rind.

Apricot Scones: Decrease butter or margarine to ¼ cup (60 mL) and add ¾ cup (175 mL) dried apricots, chopped, cooked and drained and 1 tsp. (5 mL) grated lemon rind to above recipe.

Pictured on page 69.

Currant Scones

Serve warm scones with the following Devonshire Cream recipe and assorted jams or a bowl of berries.

3 cups	flour	750 mL
¼ cup	sugar	60 mL
¼ cup	brown sugar	60 mL
½ cup	currants, washed, dried	125 mL
½ cup	butter OR margarine, chilled and cut into pieces	125 mL
¾-1 cup	whipping cream	175-250 mL

Preheat oven to 400°F (200°C). In a large bowl, combine flour, both sugars and currants. Cut butter into the flour mixture with either 2 knives or a pastry blender until mixture resembles coarse crumbs. Stir in enough cream to form a soft, slightly sticky dough. Turn dough out onto a lightly floured surface and knead until just combined. Gather dough into a ball; flatten into a round disk. Roll out to thickness of ¾" (2 cm). Cut out rounds using a 2" (5 cm) round cookie cutter. Gather scraps, reroll on floured surface and cut out additional rounds. Place scones on a well-greased cookie sheet and bake 12-15 minutes, or until puffed and golden brown. Remove from oven and cool on wire rack.

Makes 24 scones

Devonshire Cream

2 cups	sour cream	500 mL
2 tbsp.	icing (confectioner's) sugar	30 mL
1 tsp.	vanilla	5 mL

In a small bowl, combine all ingredients. Stir well to combine. Serve immediately, or can be refrigerated for up to 2 days.

Orange and Raisin Scones

2 cups	flour	500 mL
⅓ cup	sugar	75 mL
4 tsp.	baking powder	20 mL
¼ tsp.	salt	1 mL
1	orange, grated rind of	1
½ tsp.	ground nutmeg	2 mL
¼ cup	butter OR margarine, chilled	60 mL
1 cup	raisins, washed, dried	250 mL
1	egg	1
⅓ cup	EACH, milk, orange juice	75 mL
4 oz.	cream cheese, cut into cubes	125 g
1 tsp.	milk	5 mL
	sugar for topping	

In a large bowl, combine first 6 ingredients. With a pastry blender, cut in cold butter, mixture will be crumbly. Stir in raisins. In a small bowl, beat egg; add milk and orange juice; mix into dry ingredients. Add cream cheese a few pieces at a time. Dough will be soft. Turn onto a floured surface and knead 6-8 times. Press dough into a greased 9" (23 cm) pie plate. Brush with teaspoon (5 mL) of milk and sprinkle generously with sugar. Bake at 425°F (220°C) for 15-17 minutes, until light golden brown. Serve warm with jam.

Makes 8-12 scones

Scottish Oat Scones

1½ cups	flour	375 mL
1¼ cups	oatmeal	300 mL
¼ cup	sugar	60 mL
1 tbsp.	baking powder	15 mL
1 tsp.	cream of tartar	5 mL
½ tsp.	salt	2 mL
⅔ cup	melted butter OR margarine	150 mL
⅓ cup	milk	75 mL
1	egg, beaten	1
½ cup	raisins, washed, dried	125 mL

Scottish Oat Scones *(continued)*

Preheat oven to 450°F (230°C). In a large bowl, combine flour, oatmeal, sugar, baking powder, cream of tartar and salt. Stir well to combine. In a small bowl, combine melted butter, milk and beaten egg; add to dry ingredients and stir until just moistened. Mix in raisins. Shape dough into a ball. Place on a lightly floured work surface and pat out to form a ¾" (2 cm) thick circle. Transfer to a well-greased cookie sheet. Using a sharp knife, cut into 12 wedges. Bake 12-15 minutes, or until light brown. Remove from oven and transfer to wire rack. Serve warm with butter and preserves or honey.

Makes 12 scones

Herbed Scones

1¾ cups	flour	425 mL
4 tsp.	baking powder	20 mL
1 tbsp.	sugar	15 mL
1 tbsp.	chopped chives OR green onions	15 mL
1 tbsp.	chopped fresh parsley	15 mL
1 tbsp.	chopped fresh dillweed	15 mL
¾ tsp.	salt	3 mL
½ tsp.	dried thyme	2 mL
¼ cup	cold butter, cut into chunks	60 mL
1 cup	plain yogurt	250 mL

Preheat oven to 425°F (220°C). In large bowl, mix together flour, baking powder, sugar, chives, parsley, dillweed, salt and thyme. Using a pastry blender or 2 knives, cut in butter until crumbly. Using a fork, stir in yogurt; knead about 5 times, or until smooth. Transfer dough onto a lightly floured surface, roll out to 1" (2.5 cm) thickness. Using a 2" (5 cm) round cutter, cut out scones and place on a greased baking sheet. Bake for 10-12 minutes, or until lightly browned.

Makes 12 scones

Pictured on page 17.

Eileen's Tea Biscuits

Wonderful cheese biscuits – serve warm with butter and jam.

1 cup	flour	250 mL
2 tsp.	baking powder	10 mL
4 tbsp.	soft butter OR margarine	60 mL
1 cup	grated Cheddar cheese	250 mL
½ cup	cold water	125 mL

In a large bowl, combine flour and baking powder. Cut in butter with a pastry blender. Stir in cheese and water with a fork just until it holds together. Drop by teaspoonfuls (5 mL) onto a greased cookie sheet. Bake at 375°F (190°C) for 10-15 minutes, or until browned.

Makes 12 biscuits

Variations:

For **Spicy Cheddar Biscuits**, add ⅛-¼ tsp. (0.5-1 mL) cayenne.

Pictured on page 121.

Raspberry Muffins

2 cups	flour	500 mL
1 cup	sugar	250 mL
1 tbsp.	baking powder	15 mL
½ tsp.	salt	2 mL
2	eggs, lightly beaten	2
1 cup	half-and-half cereal cream	250 mL
½ cup	vegetable oil	125 mL
1 tsp.	vanilla	5 mL
1½ cups	fresh or frozen raspberries (drained)	375 mL

Preheat oven to 400°F (200°C). In a large bowl, combine flour, sugar, baking powder and salt. In another bowl, beat eggs lightly and add cream, oil and vanilla; stir into dry ingredients just until moistened. Fold in raspberries. Spoon batter into 18 greased or paper-lined muffin cups. Bake for 18-20 minutes, or until golden brown.

Makes 18 muffins

Bumbleberry Muffins with Lemon Glaze

A moist multi-berry, lemon-flavored muffin with a tangy lemon topping.

2 cups	flour	500 mL
½ cup	sugar	125 mL
1 tbsp.	baking powder	15 mL
½ tsp.	salt	2 mL
1 cup	bumbleberries*, fresh or frozen	250 mL
1 tbsp.	grated lemon rind	15 mL
1	egg	1
¾ cup	milk	175 mL
⅔ cup	vegetable oil	150 mL
¼ cup	lemon juice	60 mL

Lemon Glaze:

¼ cup	icing (confectioner's) sugar	60 mL
1 tsp.	lemon juice	5 mL
2 tsp.	finely grated lemon rind	10 mL

Preheat oven to 375°F (190°C). In a large bowl, stir together flour, sugar, baking powder and salt; add berries and lemon rind; toss to combine. In a separate bowl, whisk together egg, milk, oil and lemon juice. Pour over dry ingredients; stir just until moistened. Spoon into greased or paper-lined muffin cups. Bake for 25 minutes, or until golden and tops are firm to the touch. Let cool in pan for 5 minutes; transfer to rack and let cool completely. Store in refrigerator for up to 3 days, or may be frozen without topping for up to 1 month.

Glaze: Stir together icing sugar, lemon juice and lemon rind. Drizzle over muffins.

Makes 12 muffins

* Bumbleberries are a mixture of berries, usually available frozen. You may substitute your own mixture of raspberries, blackberries, blueberries, etc.

Apple Cinnamon Muffins

Moist and delicious with walnuts, coconut and a hint of cinnamon.

1½ cups	flour	375 mL
1½ tsp.	baking soda	7 mL
¾ tsp.	salt	3 mL
1 tsp.	ground cinnamon	5 mL
2	eggs	2
1 cup	sugar	250 mL
⅓ cup	vegetable oil	75 mL
2 cups	apples, peeled, diced	500 mL
1½ cups	chopped walnuts	375 mL
¾ cup	flaked coconut	175 mL

Preheat oven 350°F (180°C). In a large bowl, combine flour, baking soda, salt and cinnamon. In another bowl, beat eggs, sugar and oil. Stir in apples, nuts and coconut. Stir into dry ingredients just until moistened. Fill 18 greased muffin cups ¾ full. Bake 25-30 minutes. Cool in pan 10 minutes. Remove to a wire rack to cool completely.

Makes 18 muffins

Strawberry Muffins

1¾ cups	flour	425 mL
1 tsp.	baking soda	5 mL
¼ tsp.	salt	1 mL
1 cup	sugar	250 mL
½ cup	chopped pecans	125 mL
2	eggs	2
½ cup	vegetable oil	125 mL
10 oz.	pkg. frozen strawberries (thawed but undrained)	283 g

Strawberry Muffins *(continued)*

Preheat oven to 350°F (180°C). In a large bowl, combine flour, baking soda, salt, sugar and pecans. In a mixer bowl, beat eggs and oil together until well blended. Add undrained strawberries, beating at lowest speed just until strawberries are partly broken up. Add flour mixture and beat at lowest speed until batter is smooth and strawberries are in small irregular pieces. Spoon batter into 24, greased, medium-sized muffin cups. Bake 30-40 minutes, or until golden brown. Remove from oven; cool 10 minutes in pan. Turn out onto a wire rack to cool completely. These freeze well.

Makes 24 muffins

Carrot Pineapple Muffins

Moist and spicy.

1 cup	sugar	250 mL
⅔ cup	vegetable oil	150 mL
2	eggs, beaten	2
1½ cups	flour	375 mL
2 tsp.	baking powder	10 mL
1 tsp.	baking soda	5 mL
1 tsp.	ground cinnamon	5 mL
½ tsp.	salt	2 mL
1 cup	grated carrots	250 mL
1 cup	drained crushed pineapple	250 mL
1 tsp.	vanilla	5 mL

Preheat oven to 375°F (190°C). In a large bowl, combine sugar, oil and beaten eggs. Beat well. Combine flour, baking powder, baking soda, cinnamon and salt and mix well. Add dry ingredients to egg mixture; stir just to moisten. Fold in carrots, pineapple and vanilla. Spoon into well-greased muffin tins. Bake for 20-25 minutes. Remove from oven and place on rack to cool. May be kept in an airtight container for 2 days, or wrap well and freeze for up to 3 months.

Makes 12 muffins

Poppy Seed and Lemon Muffins

A moist, refreshing lemon-flavored muffin.

2	lemons	2
1¼ cups	sugar	300 mL
3 cups	flour	750 mL
3 tsp.	baking powder	15 mL
1 tsp.	baking soda	5 mL
½ tsp.	salt	2 mL
3 tbsp.	poppy seeds	45 mL
2	eggs	2
1¼ cups	milk	300 mL
¼ cup	vegetable oil	60 mL

Preheat oven to 375°F (190°C). Finely grate lemon peel. Mix half of peel with 2 tbsp. (30 mL) sugar and set aside. Squeeze juice from lemons. Measure out ½ cup (125 mL) juice and stir in remaining peel. In a large bowl, combine flour, remaining sugar, baking powder, baking soda, salt and poppy seeds. Whisk eggs in a small bowl; then whisk in milk, lemon juice and oil. Milk may curdle when mixed with lemon juice. Immediately stir egg mixture into flour mixture, just until combined. Spoon batter into 12 well-greased muffin cups. Sprinkle muffins with lemon-sugar mixture. Bake 20-30 minutes; or until golden brown. Cool muffins in pan for 5 minutes, then turn out onto a cooling rack to cool completely. Store in a sealed bag or container for up to 2 days, or freeze for up to 3 months.

Makes 12 muffins

Pictured on page 51.

Spiced Pumpkin Apple Muffins with Streusel Topping

Delectable moist, spicy muffins with streusel topping. A must for your Thanksgiving or Christmas brunches.

2½ cups	flour	625 mL
2 cups	sugar	500 mL
1 tbsp.	pumpkin pie spice	15 mL
1 tsp.	baking soda	5 mL
½ tsp.	salt	2 mL
2	eggs, lightly beaten	2
1 cup	cooked, mashed or canned pumpkin	250 mL
½ cup	vegetable oil	125 mL
2 cups	peeled, finely chopped apples	500 mL

Streusel Topping:

2 tbsp.	flour	30 mL
¼ cup	sugar	60 mL
½ tsp.	ground cinnamon	2 mL
4 tsp.	butter OR margarine	20 mL
½ cup	chopped pecans	125 mL

Preheat oven to 350°F (180°C). In a large bowl, combine flour, sugar, pumpkin pie spice, baking soda and salt; set aside. In a medium bowl, combine lightly beaten eggs, pumpkin and oil. Make a well in the dry ingredients and add the liquid ingredients, stirring just until moistened. Stir in apples. Spoon batter into greased or paper-lined muffin cups, filling ¾ full.

Streusel Topping: In a small bowl, combine flour, sugar and ground cinnamon. Cut in butter until mixture is crumbly and add nuts. Sprinkle over batter.

Bake 35-40 minutes, or until golden brown.

Makes 18 muffins

Pictured on page 139.

Oatmeal Muffins

1 cup	whole-wheat flour	250 mL
¼ cup	wheat germ	60 mL
1 cup	brown sugar, packed	250 mL
1 tsp.	baking powder	5 mL
1 tsp.	baking soda	5 mL
2 tsp.	grated orange rind	10 mL
½ cup	vegetable oil	125 mL
2	eggs, lightly beaten	2
1 cup	leftover, cooked oatmeal	250 mL
½ cup	raisins, washed, dried	125 mL
½ cup	chopped dates	125 mL
1 tsp.	vanilla	5 mL

Preheat oven to 350°F (180°C). In a large bowl, combine flour, wheat germ, brown sugar, baking powder, baking soda and orange rind. Stir well to combine. In another bowl, combine oil, eggs, oatmeal, raisins, dates and vanilla; add to dry ingredients and stir just until moistened, the batter will be thick. Spoon batter into 12 greased muffin cups. Bake for 18-20 minutes, or until golden brown. Place on wire rack to cool. May be stored in refrigerator in an air-tight container for up to 3 days, or wrap well and freeze.

Makes 12 muffins

Edible Flowers

Add flavor and flair to your food with beautiful, nutritious and flavorful edible flowers. For centuries, many cultures have used flowers as food and as edible garnishes. Experiment to satisfy your eye and your palate. Sprinkle mixed green salads with blossoms; float petals or flowers on individual servings of soup or in a glass of white wine; garnish appetizers, main courses or desserts with appropriate blossoms and leaves. *See inedible flowers note on page 62.*

Apple Blossom
Anise-Hyssop – flowers and leaves
Bachelor's Button/Cornflower – flowers and leaves
Bellflower – flowers, leaves and root

continued on page 43.

Jiffy Cinnamon Rolls

An alternative to bread dough – these take less work, less fuss and less time!

2 cups	flour	500 mL
4 tsp.	baking powder	20 mL
2 tbsp.	sugar	30 mL
¼ tsp.	salt	1 mL
¼ cup	butter OR margarine	60 mL
1 cup	milk	250 mL

Brown Sugar Cinnamon Filling:

⅓ cup	butter OR margarine, softened	75 mL
1 cup	brown sugar	250 mL
3 tsp.	ground cinnamon	15 mL
⅓ cup	raisins (optional)	75 mL

Glaze or Icing:

½ cup	icing (confectioner's) sugar	125 mL
1-2 tbsp.	milk, lemon juice OR orange juice	15-30 mL

Dough: In a large bowl, combine flour, baking powder, sugar and salt. Cut in butter with pastry cutter or 2 knives until crumbly. Make a well in center. Pour milk into well. Stir to form soft dough, adding a little more milk if needed. Turn out on a lightly floured surface; knead 8-10 times. With a well-floured rolling pin, roll into a rectangle, about 12" (30 cm) long and ⅓" (8 mm) thick.

Filling: In a bowl, cream butter and brown sugar together; stir in cinnamon; spread mixture over entire surface of the rolled dough. Sprinkle raisins over top.

Working from the long side, roll up like a jelly roll. Cut roll into 12 equal slices; place each slice in a well-buttered muffin tin. Bake at 400°F (200°C) for 20-25 minutes. Turn out immediately to cool.

Glaze: Combine icing sugar and enough liquid to make a thin glaze. Drizzle over warm cinnamon rolls.

Makes 12 rolls

Plum Kuchen

A family favorite that comes from Mother Wuth. Plums are used in the traditional German Kuchen, but you may vary with other kinds of fruit.

1¼ cups	flour	300 mL
1 tsp.	baking powder	5 mL
1 tbsp.	sugar	15 mL
½ cup	butter OR margarine	125 mL
1	egg, lightly beaten	1
1 tbsp.	milk	15 mL

Plum Filling:

2-3 lbs.	prune plums, washed, halved, pitted	1-1.5 kg
1	egg, lightly beaten	1
1 cup	sour cream	250 mL
1½ tbsp.	flour	22 mL
¾ cup	sugar	175 mL

Streusel Topping:

¾ cup	sugar	175 mL
2 tbsp.	butter OR margarine	30 mL
2 tbsp.	flour	30 mL
½ tsp.	ground cinnamon	2 mL

Dough: In a large bowl, combine flour, baking powder and sugar; cut in butter with pastry blender until crumbly. In a small bowl, combine egg and milk; stir well into flour mixture. Press dough onto sides and bottom of a well-greased 9 x 13" (23 x 33 cm) pan.

Filling: Place plums on crust, cut side up. In a small bowl, combine egg, sour cream, flour and sugar. Mix well; pour over fruit.

Streusel Topping: In a small bowl, cream together sugar and butter; add flour and cinnamon; cut into the butter mixture until crumbly. Cover fruit with streusel topping. Bake at 350°F (180°C) for 45-60 minutes, until fruit is tender and topping is a delicate brown. Serve warm or cold as is, or with cream or ice cream.

Serves 12-15

Orange Pineapple Coffeecake

The irresistible flavors of orange and pineapple combine to create a moist and delicious coffeecake.

Orange Pecan Topping:

¼ cup	flour	60 mL
¼ cup	sugar	60 mL
2 tbsp.	grated orange rind	30 mL
2 tbsp.	butter OR margarine	30 mL
½ cup	chopped pecans	125 mL

Orange Pineapple Cake:

2 cups	flour	500 mL
½ cup	sugar	125 mL
2½ tsp.	baking powder	12 mL
1 tsp.	salt	5 mL
2 tbsp.	grated orange rind	30 mL
1	egg, lightly beaten	1
¼ cup	milk	60 mL
¼ cup	pineapple juice	60 mL
½ cup	orange juice	125 mL
½ cup	oil	125 mL
10 oz.	can crushed pineapple, well drained	284 mL

Topping: Blend the topping ingredients together until crumbly.

Cake: Preheat oven to 350°F (180°C). In a large bowl, mix together flour, sugar, baking powder and salt. Stir in the grated orange rind. Make a well and mix in the egg, milk, pineapple juice, orange juice, oil and crushed pineapple, just until moistened. The batter should be lumpy, as for muffins. Pour batter into a well-greased 9" (23 cm) square baking pan or angel food pan. Sprinkle the blended topping on top and bake for 30 minutes, or until golden. Remove from oven, cool in pan for 10 minutes. Transfer to rack to cool completely. May be stored in refrigerator for 3-5 days or may be frozen for up to 1 month.

Makes 1 cake

Cranberry Orange Coffeecake
with Streusel Topping

Cranberry Filling:

2 cups	fresh or frozen cranberries	500 mL
1 cup	sugar	250 mL
4 tbsp.	orange juice	60 mL
1½ tsp.	cornstarch	7 mL
1 tbsp.	cold water	15 mL

Cake Batter:

2 cups	flour	500 mL
2½ tsp.	baking powder	12 mL
½ tsp.	salt	2 mL
8 tbsp.	butter OR margarine, softened	120 mL
¾ cup	sugar	175 mL
3 tbsp.	grated orange rind	45 mL
3	eggs	3
½ cup	milk	125 mL
2 tbsp.	orange juice	30 mL

Streusel Topping:

¾ cup	brown sugar	175 mL
½ cup	flour	125 mL
1 tsp.	ground cinnamon	5 mL
½ tsp.	ground allspice	2 mL
3 tbsp.	butter OR margarine, softened	45 mL
¾ cup	pecans	175 ml

Cranberry Filling: Place cranberries, sugar and orange juice in a small saucepan. Cook over medium heat, stirring constantly, until berries start to pop, about 5-10 minutes. Dissolve cornstarch in water and add to cranberries; stir constantly until mixture thickens slightly. Remove from heat and cool to room temperature.

Cranberry Orange Coffeecake
with Streusel Topping *(continued)*

Cake: Preheat oven to 350°F (180°C). In a small bowl, combine flour, baking powder and salt.

In large bowl, cream together butter, sugar and orange rind. Add eggs 1 at a time, beating well after each addition. Stir in flour mixture, alternately with milk and orange juice, beginning and ending with flour. Set batter aside. Combine all streusel ingredients in small mixing bowl. Mix together with fork until crumbly.

To assemble: spread half of the coffeecake batter over bottom of a well-greased 9" (23 cm) springform pan. Sprinkle with half of the streusel mixture; spoon on the cranberry filling. Cover with remaining batter and sprinkle with remaining streusel mixture. Bake 50-60 minutes, or until cake tester inserted in center of cake comes out clean. Remove from oven and cool on wire rack. Serve warm or at room temperature.

Makes 1 cake

Edible Flowers

Bergamot/Bee Balm/Oswego Tea – flowers and leaves
Borage – flowers and leaves
Calendula/Pot Marigold – petals and leaves
Camellia – petals
Carnation – petals
Chives/Garlic Chives – flowers and leaves
Chrysanthemum – petals
Dandelion – petals, leaves and root
Forsythia – flowers and leaves
Geranium – petals and leaves
Hollyhock – petals and leaves
Impatiens – flowers

continued on page 49.

Whole-Wheat Orange and Raisin Coffeecake with Orange Icing

A moist, nutritious coffeecake that is easy to make.

2 cups	whole-wheat flour	500 mL
½ cup	sugar	125 mL
1 tbsp.	baking powder	15 mL
1 tsp.	ground cinnamon	5 mL
½ tsp.	salt	2 mL
1	orange, unpeeled, seeded, cut into chunks	1
2	eggs	2
½ cup	water	125 mL
¼ cup	butter OR margarine, cut up	60 mL
½ cup	raisins	125 mL

Preheat oven to 350°F (180°C). In large bowl, combine flour, sugar, baking powder, cinnamon and salt. In a blender or food processor combine orange chunks, eggs, water and butter; cover and blend until orange is finely chopped. Make a well in dry ingredients; add orange mixture, stirring just until moistened. Add raisins. Turn into a well-greased 9" (23 cm) round cake pan; bake for 40 minutes, or until cake tester inserted in the middle of cake comes out clean. Remove from oven and cool on rack.

Makes 1 cake

Orange Icing

¾ cup	icing (confectioner's) sugar	175 mL
⅛ tsp.	ground cinnamon	0.5 mL
1-2 tbsp.	orange juice	15-30 mL

In a small bowl, stir together icing sugar, cinnamon and enough juice to make an icing of drizzling consistency. Drizzle over cake.

Marbled Coffeecake

1 cup	butter OR margarine	250 mL
1 cup	sugar	250 mL
3	eggs	3
3 cups	flour	750 mL
1 tbsp.	baking powder	15 mL
1 tsp.	baking soda	5 mL
½ tsp.	salt	2 mL
1 cup	sour cream	250 mL
2 tsp.	almond extract	10 mL

Topping:

¼ cup	cocoa	60 mL
½ cup	sugar	125 mL
½ cup	chopped pecans	125 mL

Preheat oven to 350°F (180°C). In a large bowl, cream butter. Beat in sugar and eggs, 1 at a time, beating well after each addition. In a separate bowl, combine flour, baking powder, baking soda and salt. Mix sour cream and almond extract. Add flour mixture to egg mixture alternately with sour cream mixture. Pour half the batter into a well-greased 10" (25 cm) tube pan. Mix topping ingredients. Sprinkle half the mixture over the batter in the pan, add the remaining batter and sprinkle with remaining cocoa mixture. Run a knife through the batter to marble. Bake for 45-60 minutes. Remove from oven and let cool 10 minutes in pan. Remove from pan to rack and cool completely. Wrap and store in refrigerator for up to 3 days, or freeze for up to 1 month.

Makes 1 cake

Sour Cream Coffeecake with Chocolate and Walnuts

¾ cup	butter OR margarine, softened	175 mL
1½ cups	brown sugar	375 mL
3	eggs	3
2 tsp.	vanilla	10 mL
3 cups	flour	750 mL
2 tsp.	baking powder	10 mL
2 tsp.	ground cinnamon	10 mL
1½ tsp.	baking soda	7 mL
½ tsp.	ground nutmeg	2 mL
¼ tsp.	salt	1 mL
1½ cups	sour cream	375 mL
½ cup	semisweet chocolate chips	125 mL
½ cup	walnuts	125 mL
	icing (confectioner's) sugar	

Preheat oven to 350°F (180°C). In a large bowl, beat butter until creamy; add brown sugar and beat until light and fluffy. Beat in eggs and vanilla until well blended. In a large bowl, combine flour, baking powder, cinnamon, baking soda, nutmeg and salt. Add to butter mixture alternately with sour cream; beginning and ending with flour mixture. Blend well. Stir in chocolate chips and walnuts. Spoon batter into a well-greased and floured 10" (25 cm) tube pan or Bundt pan. Bake 45-50 minutes, or until cake tester inserted in center of cake comes out clean. Cool in pan for 15 minutes. Remove from pan to wire rack; cool completely. Sprinkle with icing sugar before serving. May be stored in refrigerator for up to 3 days or can be frozen for up to 1 month.

Makes 1 cake

Amaretto Fruit Bread

The delicate almond and fruit flavor makes this a true winner.

1¾ cups	flour	425 mL
1 tbsp.	baking powder	15 mL
½ tsp.	salt	2 mL
⅔ cup	sugar	150 mL
1	egg	1
¼ cup	vegetable oil	60 mL
1 cup	milk	250 mL
3 tbsp.	amaretto OR 3 tbsp. (45 mL) milk and 1 tsp. (5 mL) almond extract	45 mL
½ cup	chopped candied cherries	125 mL
½ cup	chopped glazed pineapple	125 mL
½ cup	chopped mixed peel OR mixed fruit	125 mL
½ cup	toasted slivered almonds	125 mL

Preheat oven to 350°F (180°C). In a large bowl, combine flour, baking powder, salt and sugar. Stir with a fork to combine. In a large bowl beat egg lightly and add oil, milk and amaretto; beat well. Make a well in the center of the dry ingredients and pour the egg mixture in. Immediately add the fruit and nuts. Stir just until all dry ingredients are moist. Batter will be lumpy. Turn into a greased 3 x 5 x 9" (8 x 13 x 23 cm) loaf pan. Bake for 50-55 minutes, or until a cake tester inserted in the center comes out clean. Cool on wire rack for 10 minutes, remove from pan and cool completely on wire rack. May be wrapped and kept in refrigerator for up to 2 days, or frozen for up to 3 months.

Makes 1 loaf

Apple Nut Coffee Ring

Apples, cinnamon and walnuts make up the filling for this showy bread-dough ring.

4 cups	flour, divided	1 L
½ cup	sugar	125 mL
2 tbsp.	active dry yeast (2 x 7 g env.)	30 mL
2 tsp.	salt	10 mL
¾ cup	milk	175 mL
½ cup	warm water	125 mL
½ cup	butter OR margarine	125 mL
1	egg	1
¼ cup	butter OR margarine, melted	60 mL

Apple Nut Filling:

2 cups	peeled, cored, finely chopped apples	500 mL
½ cup	chopped walnuts	125 mL
¼ cup	sugar	60 mL
2 tsp.	ground cinnamon	10 mL

Vanilla Glaze:

2 cups	icing (confectioner's) sugar	500 mL
3 tbsp.	milk	45 mL
¼ tsp.	vanilla	1 mL

In a large mixer bowl, combine 2 cups (500 mL) flour, sugar, yeast and salt. In a saucepan, combine milk, water and butter; place on low heat and warm mixture just until lukewarm (butter does not need to melt). Pour milk mixture into flour mixture and beat at low speed. Add egg; beat at high speed for 2 minutes. With wooden spoon, stir in enough remaining flour, about 1½ cups (375 mL) to make a soft dough. Knead in remaining ½ cup (125 mL) of flour. Cover tightly and refrigerate at least 2 hours or up to 3 days.

Apple Nut Filling: In a bowl, combine apples, walnuts, sugar and cinnamon. Toss together thoroughly.

Vanilla Glaze: In a bowl, combine icing sugar, milk and vanilla. Stir until smooth.

Apple Nut Coffee Ring *(continued)*

Divide dough in half. Roll out each half to a 7 x 14" (18 x 35 cm) rectangle. Brush with melted butter. Spread half of Apple Nut Filling over each rectangle. Roll up from long side, sealing edges. Place rolls, sealed edges down, in a circle shape on greased cookie sheets. For each roll, seal ends together firmly. Cut two-thirds of way into rings at 1" (2.5 cm) intervals. Turn each section on its side. Cover and let rise in a warm place until doubled in bulk, 1½-2 hours. Bake at 350°F (180°C) for 25-30 minutes, or until golden brown. When almost cool, drizzle with Vanilla Glaze.

Makes 2 rings

Edible Flowers

Johnny-Jump-Up/Viola – flowers and leaves
Lavender – flowers
Lilac – flowers and leaves
Lilies – flowers; Day Lilies – flowers, stems, buds and roots
Note: Lily-of-the-Valley is poisonous
Marigold – petals
Mustard – flowers
Nasturtium – buds, flowers and leaves
Orange Blossoms – Petals
Pansy – flowers, stems and leaves
Peony – flowers and roots
Periwinkle/Myrtle – flowers and leaves
Poppy NOT Opium poppy – flowers, petals
Rose – flowers and hips

continued on page 58.

Cinnamon Marzipan Coffeecake

A pretzel-shaped, almond-filled, rich, yeast-dough coffeecake.

½ cup	warm milk	125 mL
1 tbsp.	active dry yeast (7 g env.)	15 mL
1 tbsp.	sugar	15 mL
3	egg yolks, beaten	3
1 cup	whipping cream	250 mL
3¼ cups	flour	770 mL
¼ cup	sugar	60 mL
1 tsp.	salt	5 mL
½ cup	butter OR margarine	125 mL

Almond Cinnamon Filling:

1 cup	almond paste	250 mL
½ cup	chopped almonds	125 mL
½ cup	sugar	125 mL
1	egg white	1
1 tsp.	ground cinnamon	5 mL
1 tsp.	almond extract	5 mL

In a small bowl, combine milk, yeast, sugar, egg yolks and cream. Let stand 10 minutes. In a large bowl, combine flour, sugar and salt; cut in butter until crumbly. Stir in liquid ingredients until just moistened. Cover with plastic wrap; refrigerate for 12-24 hours.

Filling: In a small bowl, combine almond paste, almonds, sugar, egg white, cinnamon and almond extract. Mix well and set aside. Remove dough from refrigerator; knead lightly until smooth; add more flour if necessary. Place on a well-floured surface; roll out with rolling pin to a 12 x 36" (30 x 91 cm) rectangle. Spread with filling to cover, leaving a 1" (2.5 cm) border on all sides. Roll up, like a jelly roll, starting with 1 long edge; seal. Shape into a pretzel shape. Place on a lightly greased cookie sheet. Brush with egg white; sprinkle with sliced almonds and sugar. Cover; let rise 45-60 minutes. Bake at 375°F (190°C) 25-35 minutes, or until golden brown. Remove from oven, cool 5 minutes in pan; transfer to cooling rack. Serve warm or cold. Freezes for up to 6 weeks.

Makes 1 large loaf or 2 small

Pictured on page 139.

Mother's Day Brunch

Morning Orange Drink, page 156*

Creamy Blueberry Soup, page 78

Make-Ahead Eggs Benedict, page 96*

French Toast Deluxe, page 21

Poppy Seed and Lemon Muffins, page 36*

Fast Fudge Cake, page 154

* *Pictured recipes*

   Morning Orange Drink
   Make-Ahead Eggs Benedict
   Poppy Seed and Lemon Muffins

Sticky Cinnamon Buns *(Bread Machine)*

1½ tsp.	active dry yeast	7 mL
2 cups	flour	500 mL
2 tbsp.	sugar	30 mL
2 tbsp.	butter OR margarine	30 mL
½ tsp.	salt	2 mL
2	eggs	2
½ cup	water	125 mL

Topping and Filling:

6 tbsp.	butter OR margarine, softened, divided	90 mL
¾ cup	brown sugar	175 mL
1 cup	chopped pecans (optional)	250 mL
½ cup	pancake syrup OR honey	125 mL
1 tsp.	ground cinnamon	5 mL
¾ cup	raisins	175 mL

Add all ingredients for the dough in the order suggested by your bread machine manual. Process on the basic dough cycle according to the manufacturer's directions.

Preheat oven to 350°F (180°C). At the end of the dough cycle, remove the dough from the machine. Grease 2, 9 x 11" (23 x 28 cm) baking dishes heavily with 4 tbsp. (60 mL) of the softened butter from the topping ingredients. Sprinkle 2 tbsp. (30 mL) of the brown sugar and half of the pecans over the butter in each pan. Drizzle the pancake syrup or honey equally over the 2 pans.

On a floured surface with a floured rolling pin, roll dough into a 9 x 18" (23 x 45 cm) rectangle. Butter the entire surface of the dough with the remaining 2 tbsp. (30 mL) of butter; sprinkle ¼ cup (60 mL) of the brown sugar, the cinnamon and the raisins over the buttered dough. Roll up jelly-roll fashion from 1 of the long sides. (You can freeze the buns at this point and bake them later.)

Cut the dough into 18, 1" (2.5 cm) slices. Place rolls, cut side-down, in the prepared baking dishes. Let rise 20-30 minutes. Bake 20 minutes; remove from oven. Invert baking pans immediately onto platters.

Makes 18 large buns

Jo's Hot Cross Buns

3 cups	milk	750 mL
1 cup	sugar	250 mL
1 tsp.	salt	5 mL
2 tsp.	cinnamon	10 mL
½ cup	butter OR margarine, melted	125 mL
3	eggs, beaten	3
1 cup	lukewarm water	250 mL
1 tsp.	sugar	5 mL
1 tbsp.	dry active yeast (7 oz. env.)	15 mL
6-8 cups	flour	1.5-2 L
2 cups	mixed candied fruit	500 mL

Glaze:

¼ cup	hot water	60 mL
3 tbsp.	sugar	45 mL

In a large saucepan, over medium-low heat, heat the milk until very hot to the touch, but do not boil. Remove from heat and add the sugar, salt and cinnamon. Stir to dissolve; stir in the melted butter. Let cool to lukewarm. Add the beaten eggs. In a separate small bowl, stir lukewarm water and 1 tsp. (5 mL) sugar to dissolve sugar. Sprinkle yeast on top and let stand for 15 minutes; stir down yeast and add to the milk mixture. Pour the milk mixture into a large bread bowl; add 6 cups (1.5 L) flour and candied fruit. Mix and knead, adding more flour as necessary until a firm dough has formed. Place dough in a greased bowl, twice the size of the dough. Grease the top of the dough, cover with a clean tea towel and let rise in a warm place, away from drafts, until double in size; about 1-1½ hours. Punch down; form into buns and place on greased cookie sheets. Cover with tea towel and let rise in a warm place until double in size. Preheat oven to 375°F (190°C). Bake for 15-20 minutes, or until nicely browned.

In a small bowl, combine hot water and sugar; stir until dissolved. Brush over warm buns. Place buns on wire rack to cool. When cool, drizzle icing, page 39, to form a cross on each bun.

Makes 30 buns

Salads

Fresh Fruit

Fruit & Greens

Vegetable

Main Course

Pasta

Champagne Fruit Cups

A sparkling introduction to any brunch.

19 oz.	can pineapple chunks, undrained water	540 mL
⅔ cup	chopped dried apricots	150 mL
⅓ cup	golden raisins, washed, dried	75 mL
1	pink grapefruit, peeled, cut into sections	1
2	oranges, peeled, cut into sections	2
2 cups	sliced strawberries	500 mL
1 cup	EACH, halved red and green grapes	250 mL
1	red apple, chopped	1
3 cups	ginger ale OR champagne, chilled	750 mL

Drain pineapple; reserve juice in measuring cup; add water to make 1½ cups (375 mL). In a saucepan, combine pineapple juice and water mixture, dried apricots and raisins. Simmer over low heat for 15 minutes; transfer to a bowl and cool. When cold, add pineapple, grapefruit and orange sections, strawberries, grapes and apple.

To serve, fill 8 stemmed glasses ¾ full with fruit mixture. Fill with ginger ale or champagne.

Serves 8

Four Fruit Compote

19 oz.	can pineapple chunks	540 mL
½ cup	sugar	125 mL
2 tbsp.	cornstarch	30 mL
⅓ cup	orange juice	75 mL
1 tbsp.	lemon juice	15 mL
10 oz.	can mandarin oranges, drained	284 mL
4	unpeeled apples, chopped	4
3	bananas, peeled, sliced	3

Four Fruit Compote *(continued)*

Drain pineapple, reserving ¾ cup (175 mL) juice. In a saucepan, combine sugar and cornstarch. Add the reserved pineapple juice, orange juice and lemon juice. Cook and stir over medium heat until thickened and bubbly; cook and stir 1 minute longer. Remove from heat; set aside. In a large bowl, combine pineapple chunks, oranges, apples and bananas. Pour warm sauce over the fruit. Stir gently to coat. Cover and refrigerate for 4-6 hours before serving.

Serves 10-12

Symphony of Fresh Fruits

This colorful salad is a real eye-catcher and it tastes as good as it looks.

½ cup	orange juice	125 mL
¼ cup	lemon juice	60 mL
¼ cup	brown sugar	60 mL
½ tsp.	grated orange peel	2 mL
½ tsp.	grated lemon peel	2 mL
1	cinnamon stick	1
2 cups	pineapple chunks	500 mL
1 cup	seedless red OR green grapes	250 mL
2	medium bananas, sliced	2
2	medium oranges, sectioned	2
1	medium grapefruit, sectioned	1
2 cups	sliced strawberries	500 mL
2	kiwi, peeled, sliced	2

In a medium saucepan, combine juices, sugar, orange and lemon peel and cinnamon stick; bring to a boil. Reduce heat and simmer, uncovered, for 5 minutes. Remove from heat; cool completely. Meanwhile, layer fruit in a 4-quart (4 L) glass serving bowl. Remove cinnamon stick from the sauce; pour sauce over fruit. Cover and chill for several hours.

Serves 6-8

Easy Fruit Salad with Poppy Seed Dressing

10 oz.	can mandarin orange segments, drained	284 mL
2 cups	sliced strawberries	500 mL
2 cups	peeled, sliced kiwi	500 mL
1 cup	red seedless grapes	250 mL
14 oz.	can pineapple chunks, drained	398 mL

Poppy Seed Dressing:

½ cup	mayonnaise	125 mL
½ cup	plain yogurt	125 mL
2 tbsp.	liquid honey	30 mL
1 tsp.	grated orange rind	5 mL
1 tbsp.	poppy seeds	15 mL
1	head Boston lettuce	1

In a large bowl, combine orange sections, strawberry slices, kiwi slices, grapes and pineapple; toss to combine. Set aside.

Poppy Seed Dressing: In a small bowl, combine all ingredients and mix well.

To serve, place a large lettuce leaf on each salad plate. Arrange fruit on lettuce and drizzle with dressing.

Serves 4-6

Edible Flowers

Rosemary
Runner Bean – flowers
Sage/Clary Sage/Pineapple Sage – flowers and leaves
Scented Geranium
Snapdragon – flowers

continued on page 59.

Salad Supreme

The combination of red and green grapes and blue cheese does wonders for your taste buds.

1	head romaine lettuce	1
1 cup	red seedless grapes	250 mL
1 cup	green seedless grapes	250 mL
½ cup	thinly sliced red onion	125 mL
¼ cup	olive oil	60 mL
1 tbsp.	wine vinegar	15 mL
1 tbsp.	lemon juice	15 mL
2 tsp.	Dijon mustard	10 mL
2 tsp.	honey	10 mL
½ tsp.	freshly ground pepper	2 mL
½ cup	coarsely crumbled blue cheese*	125 mL
8	slices bacon, cooked crisp, crumbled	8

Wash lettuce and tear into bite-sized pieces. Place in a large bowl; add grapes and onion and toss to combine. Whisk together, oil, vinegar, lemon juice, mustard, honey and pepper. Toss salad with dressing. Sprinkle with cheese and crumbled bacon.

Serves 4-6

* Blue cheeses vary considerably, try Danish blue or French bleu, Gorgonzola, Roquefort, Stilton, Cambozola or Danabeu. If blue cheeses are not your favorite, try crumbled feta cheese instead.

Edible Flowers

Squash Blossoms – flowers
Tuberous Begonia
Tulip – flowers and bulbs
Zucchini Blossoms – flowers

continued on page 62.

Strawberry and Cheese Salad

A colorful toss of greens and strawberries in a poppy seed dressing.

Poppy Seed Dressing:

½ cup	vegetable oil	125 mL
⅓ cup	sugar	75 mL
¼ cup	cider vinegar	60 mL
2 tsp.	poppy seeds	10 mL
¼ tsp.	salt	1 mL
⅛ tsp.	nutmeg	0.5 mL

Salad:

8 cups	torn romaine lettuce	2 L
4 cups	torn Boston lettuce	1 L
1½ cups	sliced fresh strawberries	375 mL
1 cup	shredded mozzarella cheese	250 mL
½ cup	toasted chopped pecans (optional)	125 mL

Combine the oil, sugar, vinegar, poppy seeds, salt and nutmeg in a jar with a tight-fitting lid; shake well. Just before serving, tear salad greens into a large salad bowl; add strawberries, cheese and pecans. Toss to combine well. Drizzle with dressing and toss again.

Serves 6-8

Variation:

For a flavor and color variation substitute crumbled blue cheese, see note on page 59, or feta cheese for the mozzarella.

Pictured on page 17.

Jacquie's Vegetable and Sprout Salad with Buttermilk Dressing

This salad is for the sprout lover. The red cabbage makes it colorful and the dressing is tangy and creamy.

4 cups	torn romaine lettuce	1 L
4 cups	torn iceberg lettuce	1 L
2 cups	shredded red cabbage	500 mL
1½ cups	alfalfa sprouts	375 mL
4	green onions, chopped	4
2 cups	sliced fresh mushrooms	500 mL
½ cup	chopped celery	125 mL
½ cup	peeled, chopped cucumbers	125 mL

Creamy Buttermilk Dressing:

½ cup	ranch-style dressing	125 mL
½ cup	mayonnaise	125 mL
¼ cup	buttermilk	60 mL

In a large salad bowl, combine the torn romaine and iceberg lettuce; add red cabbage, alfalfa sprouts, onions, mushrooms, celery and cucumbers. Mix and toss well to combine. Set aside. In a small bowl, combine the ranch dressing, mayonnaise and buttermilk. Stir well to combine. Just before serving, pour dressing over salad and toss well to combine.

Serves 8-10

Torn Spinach Salad

Garlic Red Wine Dressing:

2	garlic cloves, minced	2
2 tbsp.	red wine vinegar	30 mL
1 tsp.	sugar	5 mL
1 tsp.	salt	5 mL
1 tsp.	dry mustard	5 mL
½ tsp.	pepper	2 mL
1 tbsp.	Worcestershire sauce	15 mL
6 tbsp.	vegetable oil	90 mL
8 cups	torn crisp young spinach, (hard stems removed) 2-2½ lbs. (1-1.25 kg)	2 L
3	hard-boiled eggs, sliced	3
8	slices bacon, fried crisp, crumbled	8
3	green onions, finely chopped	3
2 cups	sliced fresh mushrooms	500 mL
1 cup	sliced fresh cauliflower	250 mL

Dressing: Combine garlic, vinegar, sugar, salt, dry mustard, pepper, Worcestershire sauce and oil in a shaker jar or bowl and mix well to combine. Refrigerate.

Prepare remaining ingredients and combine in a large salad bowl. Just before serving, shake dressing again and pour over salad.

Serves 6-8

Inedible Flowers

WARNING:
Make sure that edible flowers have not been sprayed with pesticides.

DO NOT EAT THE FOLLOWING FLOWERS:
Aconite (Monkshood), Anemone, Azalea, Belladonna, Bleeding Heart, Buttercup, Clematis, Daffodil, Datura, Delphinium, Hyacinths, Jasmine (yellow), Larkspur, Lily-of-the-Valley, Lobelia, Lupine, Morning Glory, Oleander, Petunia, Poppy (red), Rhododendron, Rose (Christmas), Snowdrop, Spurge, Tobacco, Wisteria.

Greek Salad

1	head romaine lettuce, torn into bite-size pieces	1
2	tomatoes, cut into wedges	2
1	English cucumber, sliced	1
1	red onion, thinly sliced	1
1½ cups	Greek black olives, drained	375 mL
8 oz.	feta cheese, crumbled	250 g
4 tbsp.	olive oil	60 mL
4 tbsp.	red wine vinegar	60 mL
1 tsp.	dried oregano	5 mL
¼ tsp.	pepper	1 mL

Spread lettuce on a large platter. Arrange tomatoes, cucumber, onion, olives and cheese on lettuce. In a small bowl, whisk together oil, vinegar, oregano and pepper. Pour dressing over salad. Toss to coat.

Serves 6

Broccoli Bacon Salad

Try this crunchy salad with roast pork, baked ham, grilled chicken – anything!

1	large bunch broccoli, in florets	1
1	small red onion, coarsely chopped	1
1	carrot, thinly sliced	1
10-12	slices bacon, cooked, crumbled	10-12
4 tbsp.	vinegar	60 mL
½ cup	mayonnaise	125 mL

In a large serving bowl, combine broccoli, onion, carrots and bacon; set aside. In a small bowl, combine vinegar and mayonnaise. Just before serving, pour dressing over broccoli mixture; toss to coat.

Serves 6-8

Pictured on page 69.

Marinated Vegetable Salad

Marinating the vegetables overnight gives this fresh salad terrific flavor.

5 cups	broccoli florets	1.25 L
2	cucumbers, peeled, sliced	2
1	red onion, thinly sliced	1
1	green pepper, seeded, thinly sliced	1
1	red pepper, seeded, thinly sliced	1
3	carrots, peeled, thinly sliced	3
¾ cup	black olives, drained, sliced	175 g
½ cup	grated Parmesan cheese	125 mL
1 tsp.	minced fresh parsley	5 mL
½ tsp.	EACH, dried oregano, basil	2 mL
1 cup	Italian dressing	250 mL
12	cherry tomatoes, halved	12

Combine all ingredients, except cherry tomatoes, in a large bowl. Cover and refrigerate overnight, stirring occasionally. When ready to serve, add tomatoes and toss. If desired, season with salt and pepper.

Serves 6-8

Pictured on page 103.

Parmesan Vegetable Toss

1 cup	EACH, mayonnaise, sour cream	250 mL
½ tsp.	prepared mustard	2 mL
¾ cup	grated Parmesan cheese	175 mL
½ tsp.	dried basil	2 mL
4 cups	EACH, broccoli, cauliflower florets	1 L
2 cups	coin-sliced carrots	500 mL
1	yellow pepper, seeded, sliced	1
½	medium red onion, sliced	½
8 oz.	can sliced water chestnuts, drained	227 g
1	large head iceberg lettuce, torn	1
12-14	slices bacon, cooked, crumbled	12-14
2 cups	croûtons (optional)	500 mL

Parmesan Vegetable Toss *(continued)*

In a large bowl, combine mayonnaise, sour cream, mustard, Parmesan and basil. Add broccoli, cauliflower, carrots, pepper, onion and water chestnuts; toss. Cover; refrigerate for several hours or overnight. Just before serving, place lettuce in a bowl and top with vegetable mixture. Sprinkle with bacon. Top with croûtons if desired.

Serves 10-12

Bean Salad with Tangy Dressing

This tangy salad is great for a barbecue buffet.

19 oz.	can cut green beans, drained	540 mL
19 oz.	can cut yellow wax beans, drained	540 mL
19 oz.	can garbanzo beans, drained	540 mL
19 oz.	can red kidney beans, drained	540 mL
1	red onion, sliced	1
1	green pepper, chopped	1
¾ cup	chopped celery	175 mL
14 oz.	can whole baby corn, drained	398 mL
¾ cup	sugar	175 mL
½ cup	vegetable oil	125 mL
½ cup	vinegar	125 mL
1 tsp.	salt	5 mL
1 tsp.	celery seed	5 mL
¼ tsp.	pepper	1 mL

Drain beans; place in a large bowl; add onion, pepper, celery and corn.

Combine the sugar, oil, vinegar, salt, celery seed and pepper in a saucepan over medium-high heat; boil for 2 minutes. Remove from heat; let cool and pour over vegetables. Let stand 24 hours, stirring several times.

Serves 15-20

Italian Salad

This hearty salad is a meal in itself. Serve it with a loaf of Italian bread.

1	head romaine lettuce, torn	1
4	tomatoes, chopped	4
1	green pepper, seeded, chopped	1
4 oz.	salami, diced	115 g
1 cup	garbanzo beans	250 mL
4 oz.	mozzarella cheese, diced	115 g
½ cup	sliced, pitted black olives	125 mL
½ cup	green olives, sliced	125 mL

Basil and Lemon Dressing:

¾ cup	olive oil	175 mL
2 tbsp.	red wine vinegar	30 mL
1 tsp.	dried basil	5 mL
1 tbsp.	Dijon mustard	15 mL
2 tsp.	fresh lemon juice	10 mL
½ tsp.	sugar	2 mL
½ tsp.	salt	2 mL
⅛ tsp.	pepper	0.5 mL

Tear lettuce into a large salad bowl and add tomatoes, pepper, salami, garbanzo beans, cheese, black and green olives. In a jar with a tight-fitting lid, combine all the dressing ingredients. Shake well; pour over salad and toss well. Serve immediately.

Serves 4-6

Layered Chicken Salad

A real winner on warm days. This salad has a unique blend of vegetables. It makes a lovely presentation in a glass bowl.

4-5 cups	shredded iceberg lettuce	1-1.25 L
1	medium English cucumber, thinly sliced	1
1 cup	fresh bean sprouts	250 mL
8 oz.	can sliced water chestnuts, drained	227 g
½ cup	thinly sliced green onions	125 mL
2 cups	halved fresh snow peas	500 mL
4 cups	cubed cooked chicken	1 L
2 cups	mayonnaise	500 mL
	cherry tomatoes and fresh parsley sprigs (optional)	

Place the lettuce in the bottom of a 4-quart (4 L) glass salad bowl. Layer with cucumber, bean sprouts, water chestnuts, onions, snow peas and chicken. Spread mayonnaise over salad. Cover and chill several hours or overnight. Garnish with cherry tomatoes and parsley, if desired.

Serves 8-10

Basil

Basil has always been popular in Mediterranean cuisines and is especially identified with Italian cooking. It goes extremely well with tomatoes and it is also one of the main ingredients in pesto sauce.

The list of dishes that benefit from basil is indeed long – anything with a tomato base, bean soup, spiced meat dishes, any kind of lamb or chicken, scrambled eggs, potato salad, any green salad; and many vegetables including beans, zucchini, eggplant, carrots and cauliflower.

Shrimp and Vegetable Salad

A tangy, colorful salad, marinated overnight for the flavors to develop and ripen.

1 lb.	shrimp, peeled, deveined, cooked	500 g
1 cup	cauliflower florets	250 mL
½ lb.	small whole fresh mushrooms	250 g
¼ lb.	whole fresh snow peas	125 g
14 oz.	can whole baby corn, drained	398 mL
1	large green pepper, seeded, chopped	1
1	large red pepper, seeded, chopped	1
4	green onions, chopped	3

Lemon Dill Dressing:

¾ cup	lemon juice	175 mL
2 tsp.	sugar	10 mL
1 tsp.	salt	1 mL
½ tsp.	dried dillweed	2 mL
5 drops	hot pepper sauce	5 drops
¾ cup	vegetable oil	175 mL

In a large shallow dish combine, shrimp, cauliflower, mushrooms, snow peas, baby corn, green pepper, red pepper and green onions.

Dressing: In a small bowl or jar, combine all remaining ingredients, except the oil, and mix well. Add oil and whisk or shake well. Pour over shrimp mixture. Cover; chill 6 hours or overnight, stirring occasionally. Refrigerate leftovers.

Serves 6-8

Pictured on page 121.

Canada Day Brunch

Five-Fruit Breakfast Cocktail, page 156

Dill Pickle Soup, page 79

Smoked Salmon Strata, page 105

Ham and Shrimp Gâteau, page 112*

Broccoli Bacon Salad, page 63*

English Tea Scones – Orange Pecan variation, page 28*

Welsh Cakes, page 27

Fresh Strawberry Cheesecake, page 145

* Pictured recipes
   Ham and Shrimp Gâteau
   Broccoli Bacon Salad
   English Tea Scones – Orange Pecan Variation

Pasta and Shrimp Salad

Fresh Dill and Garlic Dressing:

6 tbsp.	coarsely chopped fresh dillweed	90 mL
3	garlic cloves, minced	3
3 tbsp.	olive oil	45 mL
3 tbsp.	lemon juice	45 mL
2 tbsp.	red wine vinegar	30 mL
½ tsp.	salt	2 mL
⅛ tsp.	pepper	0.5 mL

1 lb.	large shrimp, peeled and cooked	500 g
1½ cups	cooked baby shell pasta	375 mL
4 oz.	feta cheese, crumbled	115 g
1	large tomato, diced	1
1	green pepper, seeded, diced	1
1 cup	black olives, pitted, sliced	250 mL
½	red onion, sliced	½

lettuce leaves, dillweed sprigs and
olives for garnish

Dressing: Place dillweed in food processor; process until minced. Scrape down sides of bowl and add garlic, oil, lemon juice, vinegar, salt and pepper. Process until blended, about 5-10 seconds. Transfer dressing to a large bowl.

Salad: Add shrimp, pasta, feta cheese, tomato, green pepper, olives and onion to dressing. Toss gently to combine. Cover and refrigerate for 3 hours. To serve, mound salad decoratively on lettuce leaves. Garnish with dillweed sprigs and olives.

Serves 4

Susan's Pasta Salad

Susan, Jo's daughter, serves this colorful, creamy, salad on special occasions.

2 cups	cooked colored pasta	500 mL
1 cup	cubed ham sausage	250 mL
1 cup	drained, sliced baby corn	250 mL
1½ cups	cubed Cheddar cheese	375 mL
¾ cup	green olives, halved	175 mL
1 cup	Gherkin pickles, diagonally sliced	250 mL
1½ cups	diced red and green peppers	375 mL
4	green onions, chopped	4
1 cup	sliced baby carrots	250 mL
1 cup	sliced celery	250 mL
1 cup	sliced radishes	250 mL
15	whole cherry tomatoes	15
1 cup	sliced fresh mushrooms	250 mL

Creamy Dill Dressing:

1 cup	mayonnaise	250 mL
½ cup	green relish	125 mL
1 tbsp.	prepared mustard	15 mL
½ cup	dill pickle juice	125 mL
2 tbsp.	sugar	30 mL
½ tsp.	salt	2 mL
¼ tsp.	pepper	1 mL

Cook pasta according to package directions; drain and cool. Place pasta in a large bowl and add all other salad ingredients.

Dressing: In a small bowl combine all dressing ingredients and mix well to combine. Pour over salad; toss and serve.

Serves 8-10

Note:

 When pasta salads are "dressed" in advance and then refrigerated, the dressing is absorbed into the pasta and the flavor becomes less intense. Add dressing just before serving.

Greek Pasta Salad

4 cups	cooked pasta	1 L
1 cup	sliced, pitted Greek black olives	250 mL
1 cup	halved cherry tomatoes	250 mL
½	cucumber, quartered, sliced	½
4 oz.	feta cheese, crumbled	115 g
¼ cup	sliced green onion	60 mL
2 tbsp.	finely chopped parsley	30 mL

Greek Lemon Herb Dressing:

3 tbsp.	lemon juice	45 mL
1 tsp.	dried mint	5 mL
½ tsp.	dried oregano	2 mL
½ tsp.	dried rosemary	2 mL
½ tsp.	sugar	2 mL
¼ tsp.	salt	1 mL
¼ tsp.	pepper	1 mL
½ cup	olive oil	125 mL

In a large bowl combine cooked pasta, olives, tomatoes, cucumber, feta cheese, green onion and parsley; toss well.

Dressing: Combine all dressing ingredients in a jar with tight-fitting lid. Shake well to blend. Pour over pasta mixture. Toss well.

Serves 6-8

Parsley

The mild-flavored, curled green leaf variety we are most familiar with is called curly parsley. Use the leaves in cream sauces, herbed butter, sauces for pasta, in green salads, vegetable dishes (especially potatoes and potato salad), casseroles, omelets, scrambled eggs, or with fish and poultry. The stem, which is the most flavorful part, should be used in soups or stews.

Parsley is a popular window box herb, but it also lends itself well to drying and freezing.

Basic Vinaigrette

½ cup	vegetable oil	125 mL
⅓ cup	white wine vinegar	75 mL
1 tbsp.	sugar	15 mL
2 tsp.	fresh thyme, oregano OR basil; or ½ tsp. (2 mL) dried	10 mL
½ tsp.	paprika	2 mL
¼ tsp.	dry mustard OR 1 tsp. (5 mL) Dijon mustard	1 mL
⅛ tsp.	pepper	0.5 mL

In a screw-top jar mix oil, vinegar, sugar, herbs, paprika, mustard and pepper. Cover; shake well. Store in the refrigerator for up to 2 weeks. Shake before serving. Use on any type of green salad.

Makes ¾ cup (175 mL)

Variations:

 Red Pepper Vinaigrette: Prepare the vinaigrette as directed, except omit the herbs and add a dash of ground red pepper (cayenne).

Parmesan Vinaigrette: Prepare the vinaigrette as directed, using oregano. Add 2 tbsp. (30 mL) grated Parmesan cheese; ¼ tsp. (1 mL) celery seed and 1 garlic clove, minced.

 Red Wine Vinaigrette: Prepare the vinaigrette as directed, except decrease the vinegar to 3 tbsp. (45 mL). Use 1 tsp. (5 mL) each of fresh thyme and oregano. Add 2 tbsp. (30 mL) dry red wine and 1 garlic clove, minced.

 Garlic Vinaigrette: Prepare the vinaigrette as directed, except omit the herbs and paprika. Add 3 large garlic cloves, minced.

Soups & Chowders

Chilled Fruit
Creamy or Hearty Vegetable
Meaty Meal-in-a-Bowl

Fresh Fruit Soup

12½ oz.	can frozen orange juice concentrate, thawed, mixed with water	355 mL
1 cup	sugar	250 mL
1	cinnamon stick	1
6	whole cloves	6
¼ cup	cornstarch	60 mL
2 tbsp.	lemon juice	30 mL
2 cups	sliced fresh strawberries	500 mL
2	bananas, sliced	2
1 cup	sliced kiwi	250 mL
	fresh mint leaves	

In a large saucepan, mix orange juice with water according to package directions. Remove ½ cup (125 mL) of juice; set aside. Add sugar, cinnamon stick and cloves to saucepan; bring to a boil. Reduce heat and simmer for 5 minutes. Blend cornstarch and reserved juice to form a smooth paste; stir into pan. Bring to a boil; cook and stir until thickened, about 2 minutes more. Remove from heat and stir in lemon juice. Pour into a large bowl; cover and chill. Just before serving, remove the spices and stir in the fruit. Garnish with mint leaves.

Serves 8-10

Chilled Strawberry Soup

A cool refreshing clear strawberry flavor, this is a great summer soup.

2 cups	fresh strawberries	500 mL
½ cup	white wine	125 mL
1 tsp.	grated lemon peel	5 mL
½ cup	sugar	125 mL
2 tbsp.	lemon juice	30 mL
3	strawberries, sliced, for garnish	3

Chilled Strawberry Soup *(continued)*

Hull and wash strawberries. In a blender or food processor container, combine whole berries, wine, lemon peel, sugar and lemon juice. Blend or process until ingredients are smooth. Cover and refrigerate until well chilled. Serve chilled soup in chilled soup bowls or cups, garnished with additional sliced strawberries.

Serves 3

Creamy Strawberry Soup

10 oz.	pkg. frozen strawberries in syrup (thawed)	283 g
2 tbsp.	cornstarch	30 mL
½ cup	cold water	125 mL
1 cup	sour cream	250 mL
2 cups	half-and-half cereal cream	500 mL
4 tbsp.	strawberry-flavored liqueur OR orange juice (optional) sliced strawberries and mint leaves for garnish	60 mL

In a large saucepan over medium-high heat, bring the thawed strawberries, including syrup, to a boil. Dissolve the cornstarch in the cold water and add to the strawberry mixture, stirring constantly. Bring the mixture to a boil, reduce heat and simmer for 3 minutes, stirring constantly. Transfer the strawberry mixture to a bowl; let it cool to room temperature and whisk in the sour cream, the half-and-half cream and liqueur or orange juice. Chill the soup, covered, overnight and thin it with additional half-and-half to taste, if desired. Ladle soup into chilled bowls. Garnish with sliced strawberries and mint leaves.

Serves 4-6

Chilled Raspberry Soup

A tangy, cool, refreshing soup to use for a summer brunch.

20 oz.	pkg. frozen raspberries, thawed	568 mL
1¼ cups	water	300 mL
¼ cup	white wine	60 mL
1 cup	cran-raspberry juice	250 mL
½ cup	sugar	125 mL
1½ tsp.	ground cinnamon	7 mL
3	whole cloves	3
1 tbsp.	lemon juice	15 mL
1 cup	raspberry-flavored yogurt	250 mL
½ cup	sour cream	125 mL

In a blender or food processor, purée raspberries, water and wine. Transfer to a large saucepan; add the cran-raspberry juice, sugar, cinnamon and cloves. Bring just to a boil over medium heat. Remove from heat; strain and allow to cool. Whisk in lemon juice and yogurt. Refrigerate 4-6 hours. To serve, pour into chilled bowls or cups and top with a dollop of sour cream.

Serves 4-6

Pictured on page 17.

Creamy Blueberry Soup

Indulge guests with this elegant creamy blueberry starter soup.

⅓ cup	sour cream OR plain yogurt	75 mL
10 oz.	pkg. frozen blueberries (partially thawed)	283 g
2 tbsp.	sugar	30 mL
	lemon slices for garnish	

In a blender or food processor, process sour cream, blueberries and sugar until smooth. Cover and refrigerate until well chilled. Serve chilled soup in chilled bowls or cups garnished with lemon slices.

Serves 2

Dill Pickle Soup

We have created this soup to taste like one served at a quaint little restaurant on the west coast.

½ cup	butter OR margarine	125 mL
¼ cup	flour	60 mL
6 cups	chicken broth	1.5 L
1-1½ cups	dill pickles, shredded or finely chopped	250-375 mL
1 cup	white wine OR additional chicken broth	250 mL
1	small onion, finely chopped	1
2 tbsp.	sugar	30 mL
2 tbsp.	vinegar	30 mL
1 tbsp.	Worcestershire sauce	15 mL
6	garlic cloves, minced	6
2 tsp.	salt	10 mL
1 tsp.	dillweed	5 mL
½ tsp.	pepper	2 mL
2 cups	warm milk	500 mL
	dash green food coloring (optional)	
	croûtons (optional)	

In a large saucepan, melt butter. Add flour; cook and stir until bubbly. Gradually add the chicken broth, stirring constantly. Add all other ingredients, except for the milk. Bring to a boil over medium heat, then reduce heat to low. In a small saucepan, heat milk over medium heat until warm to the touch; add to soup. Add food coloring and garnish with croûtons, if desired. Serve immediately.

Serves 8-10

Dill

The seed of the dill plant is stronger tasting than the leaves and is used in longer cooking recipes. Use the seeds in breads, gravy, sauces, salad dressings, fish soups and beef stew.

Fresh dillweed will only last for a few days in the refrigerator, but it freezes well on the stem.

Country Borscht

Wonderful after a winter outing.

8 cups	beef stock	2 L
1	large onion, diced	1
2 cups	chopped celery	500 mL
28 oz.	can tomatoes, broken	796 mL
2	large potatoes, peeled, diced	2
2 cups	diced carrots	500 mL
1 cup	diced turnips	250 mL
1 tbsp.	vinegar	15 mL
1 cup	peas, fresh or frozen	250 mL
1 cup	green beans, fresh or frozen	250 mL
3	medium beets, peeled, diced, cooked	3
3 cups	shredded green cabbage	750 mL
2 tsp.	dried dillweed or 2 tbsp. (30 mL) fresh	10 mL
½ tsp.	salt	2 mL
⅛ tsp.	pepper	0.5 mL
	sour cream	

Beef Stock: In a large saucepan, place 3-4 meaty soup bones and cover with 8-10 cups (2-2.5 L) of cold water. Simmer over low heat for 4-5 hours, or until meat can easily be removed from the bones. Remove bones; remove meat from bones; chop and set aside. Cool the stock and remove all fat before proceeding with soup.

In a large saucepan, combine the beef stock, onion, celery, tomatoes, potatoes, carrots, turnips and vinegar. Simmer over low heat until vegetables are tender. Add peas, beans, cooked beets and cabbage. Simmer until cabbage is tender. Add dillweed, salt, pepper and meat from the beef bones and heat through, 5-10 minutes. To serve add 1 tsp. (5 mL) sour cream to each soup bowl; then add soup.

Serves 8-10

Campbell's Bean Soup

A favorite family soup served by our Aunt Susie Campbell during threshing season for lunch. Aunt Susie always added salt pork to this recipe.

4 cups	beans, use all OR any of the following combination, kidney beans, navy beans, lima beans, split green OR yellow peas, pinto beans OR lentils	1 L
	water	
1	ham bone (optional)	1
6 cups	chicken stock	1.5 L
2 cups	water OR ham stock	500 mL
28 oz.	can tomatoes, broken	796 mL
1	large onion, chopped	1
2 cups	chopped celery	500 mL
4	carrots, sliced	4
4	garlic cloves, minced	4
2 tbsp.	dried parsley	30 mL
1½ tsp.	dried thyme	7 mL
½ tsp.	turmeric	2 mL
½ tsp.	salt	2 mL
10 drops	hot pepper sauce	10 drops

Prepare beans as per instructions on page 89. Drain beans; (remove ham bone if using bone) add all remaining ingredients. Simmer for 2-3 hours, or until beans and vegetables are tender. Serve immediately.

Serves 12-15

Dillweed

This medium-flavored herb adds a nice tang to many dishes. The soft, feathery dark green leaves of the plant are called dillweed. It is delicious with all fish, but is especially a classic with salmon, It also goes well with eggs, pork, lamb, poultry or veal. It complements vegetables such as cabbage, potatoes, carrots, cauliflower, green beans, squash and cucumbers. Use as seasoning in salads, cream soups, sauces, spreads and dips. Add dillweed toward the end of the cooking period as its flavor does not survive well under prolonged heat.

Alberta Bounty Vegetable Soup

A savory soup full of nutritious vegetables.

10 cups	chicken stock	2.5 L
2	large carrots, chopped	2
1	large onion, finely chopped	1
1 cup	chopped celery	250 mL
2 cups	shredded cabbage	500 mL
1 tsp.	dried thyme	5 mL
1	bay leaf	1
1 cup	uncooked macaroni	250 mL
1 cup	EACH, frozen peas, lima beans	250 mL
19 oz.	can tomatoes, coarsely chopped	540 mL
½ tsp.	salt	2 mL
6-8 drops	hot pepper sauce	6-8 drops
	grated Parmesan cheese	

In a large saucepan, combine chicken stock, carrots, onion, celery, cabbage, thyme and bay leaf; bring to a boil; reduce heat and simmer for 15 minutes. Add the macaroni and simmer for 15 minutes, or until macaroni is tender. Stir in frozen peas, lima beans and tomatoes; simmer 5 minutes. Remove bay leaf; add salt and hot pepper sauce. Serve immediately, topped with grated Parmesan cheese.

Serves 8-10

Fresh Tomato Soup

A full-bodied tomato soup. Serve with crackers or rolls.

¼ cup	water	60 mL
8 cups	quartered fresh, ripe tomatoes	2 L
1 tbsp.	butter OR margarine	15 mL
⅛ tsp.	baking soda	0.5 mL
2 cups	milk	500 mL
2 tsp.	dillweed	10 mL
½ tsp.	salt	2 mL
⅛ tsp.	pepper	0.5 mL

Fresh Tomato Soup *(continued)*

In a large saucepan, simmer water and tomatoes over low heat until tomatoes are tender and skin and pulp separate. Remove from heat. Put tomatoes through sieve to remove skin and seeds. Discard pulp and return liquid to heat. Add butter, baking soda, milk, dillweed, salt and pepper. Heat over low heat, do not boil. Serve immediately.

Serves 4-6

Zesty Pumpkin Soup

¼ cup	butter OR margarine	60 mL
1 cup	chopped onion	250 mL
2	garlic cloves, minced	2
1 tsp.	curry powder	5 mL
½ tsp.	salt	2 mL
¼ tsp.	coriander	1 mL
⅛ tsp.	crushed red pepper	0.5 mL
3 cups	chicken stock	750 mL
19 oz.	can pumpkin	540 mL
1 cup	half-and-half cereal cream	250 mL
	sour cream and chives (optional)	

In a large saucepan, over medium-low heat, melt butter and sauté onion and garlic until soft. Add curry powder, salt, coriander and red pepper; cook for 1 minute. Add stock; boil gently, uncovered for 15-20 minutes. Stir in pumpkin and half-and-half cream; cook for 5 minutes. Pour into blender container. Cover and blend until creamy. Serve warm or reheat to desired temperature. If desired, garnish with a dollop of sour cream and chopped chives.

Serves 4-6

Pictured on page 103.

Cream of Potato Soup

1	large onion, finely chopped	1
2 cups	milk	500 mL
1½ cups	cooked, mashed potatoes	375 mL
2 tbsp.	butter OR margarine	30 mL
2 tbsp.	flour	30 mL
2 cups	milk	500 mL
1 tsp.	chopped parsley	5 mL
¼ tsp.	EACH, celery salt, salt	1 mL
⅛ tsp.	pepper	0.5 mL

In a small saucepan, over medium heat, cook onion in a small amount of water until tender. Add 2 cups (500 mL) of milk; heat until hot but not boiling. In a large saucepan, add milk and onions gradually to mashed potatoes; set aside. In a small saucepan, over medium heat, melt butter; add flour, stirring constantly. Gradually add remaining 2 cups (500 mL) of milk to make a thin white sauce. Cook and stir for 1-2 minutes; add to the potato mixture. Stir in parsley, celery salt, salt and pepper. Heat for 10-15 minutes; stir occasionally. Serve immediately.

Serves 4-6

Mushroom and Potato Chowder

Thick, creamy and flavorful, this soup is a meal in a bowl.

1	large onion, chopped	1
¼ cup	butter OR margarine	60 mL
2 tbsp.	flour	30 mL
1 tsp.	salt	5 mL
½ tsp.	pepper	2 mL
3 cups	beef stock	750 mL
1 lb.	fresh mushrooms, sliced	500 g
1 cup	chopped celery	250 mL
1 cup	peeled, diced potatoes	250 mL
1 cup	half-and-half cereal cream	250 mL
¼ cup	grated Parmesan cheese	60 mL

Mushroom and Potato Chowder *(continued)*

In a large kettle, sauté onion in butter until tender. Add flour, salt and pepper; stir to make a smooth paste. Gradually add beef stock, stirring constantly. Bring to a boil; cook and stir for 1 minute. Add the mushrooms, celery and potatoes. Reduce heat; cover and simmer for 30 minutes, until vegetables are tender. Add cream and Parmesan cheese; heat through.

Serves 4-6

Cheesy Baked Potato Soup

A creamy flavorful soup using leftover baked potatoes

½ cup	butter OR margarine	125 mL
2	garlic cloves, minced	2
1	large onion, chopped	1
1 cup	sliced fresh mushrooms	250 mL
½ cup	flour	125 mL
6 cups	milk	1.5 L
6	medium baking potatoes, baked, cooled, peeled, cubed (4 cups [1 L])	6
1 tbsp.	dried parsley	15 mL
12	strips bacon, cooked, crumbled	12
1¼ cups	shredded Cheddar cheese	300 mL
½ cup	sour cream	125 mL
¾ tsp.	salt	3 mL
⅛ tsp.	pepper	0.5 mL

In a large saucepan, melt the butter over medium-low heat and sauté garlic, onion and mushrooms until tender. Stir in flour; stir constantly until smooth. Gradually add milk, stirring constantly until thickened. Add potatoes and parsley. Bring to a boil, stirring constantly. Reduce heat; simmer for 10 minutes. Add bacon, cheese, sour cream, salt and pepper. Stir until cheese is melted. Serve immediately, topped with additional grated cheese and crumbled bacon.

Serves 8-10

Savory Cheese Soup

A delicious creamy soup. The big cheese flavor blends wonderfully with the vegetables.

3 tbsp.	butter OR margarine	45 mL
1	small onion, chopped	1
4	garlic cloves, minced	4
¼ cup	flour	60 mL
¼ tsp.	salt	1 mL
⅛ tsp.	pepper	0.5 mL
2 cups	half-and-half cereal cream	500 mL
2 cups	chicken stock	500 mL
1 cup	chopped cauliflower	250 mL
1 cup	chopped broccoli	250 mL
½ cup	finely chopped celery	125 mL
1½ cups	shredded Cheddar cheese	375 mL
¾ cup	shredded mozzarella cheese	175 mL
	fresh or dried chives (optional)	

In a large saucepan, melt butter and sauté onion and garlic until tender. Add flour, salt and pepper; stir until smooth. Gradually add half-and-half cream; cook and stir over medium heat until thickened and bubbly. Meanwhile, bring chicken stock to a boil in a small saucepan. Add cauliflower, broccoli and celery; simmer for 5 minutes, or until vegetables are tender. Add to cream mixture and stir until blended. Add cheeses. Cook and stir until melted, do not boil. Garnish with chives, if desired.

Serves 4

Herbal Mythology

The Romans used to weave dillweed flower heads into crowns to recognize heroism.

In India, basil is sacred. The legend is that the wife of the god Vishnu came to earth in the form of this plant. Prayers of apology are offered whenever it is necessary to cut the plant.

Chunky Corn Chowder

½ lb.	bacon	250 g
1	medium-sized onion, chopped	1
2	garlic cloves, minced	2
¼ cup	flour	60 mL
2 cups	chicken stock	500 mL
3 cups	milk	750 mL
2 cups	whole-kernel corn	500 mL
14 oz.	can cream-style corn	398 mL
¼ tsp.	salt	1 mL
⅛ tsp.	pepper	0.5 mL
½ tsp.	turmeric	2 mL
1 tbsp.	dried parsley	15 mL
6-8 drops	hot pepper sauce	6-8 drops
2	small potatoes, peeled, cubed	2

In a large saucepan, cook bacon until crisp. Remove bacon; crumble and set aside. In the drippings, sauté onion and garlic until tender. Add flour; cook and stir until bubbly. Cook 1 minute longer. Gradually stir in chicken stock and milk; bring to a boil. Reduce heat; cook and stir until thickened. Add corn, salt, pepper, turmeric, parsley and hot pepper sauce. In a small saucepan, over medium heat, cook the potatoes in just enough water to cover, until tender. Add potatoes to the chowder and cook for an additional 10 minutes, or until heated through. Sprinkle with bacon and serve immediately.

Serves 6-8

Pictured on page 121.

Herbal Mythology

- It was once believed that fairies made their homes in the thyme patch.
- Ancient Romans fed parsley to the horses before a chariot race to give them stamina.
- Ancient Greeks considered parsley a symbol of honor, as it was believed that parsley grew where a hero's blood was shed.

Aunt Agnes's New England Crab and Corn Chowder

Our mother's sister, Agnes, moved to the New England coast and this soon became one of her favorite recipes.

1 tbsp.	butter OR margarine	15 mL
1	large onion, finely chopped	1
3	garlic cloves, minced	3
1 cup	whole-kernel corn, canned or frozen	250 mL
2 cups	chicken stock	500 mL
1 cup	half-and-half cereal cream	250 mL
¼ tsp.	salt	1 mL
⅛ tsp.	pepper	0.5 mL
1 cup	peeled, chopped potato	250 mL
½ cup	seeded, finely chopped red pepper	125 mL
½ cup	chopped celery	125 mL
14 oz.	can cream-style corn	398 mL
8 oz.	fresh or frozen, cooked crab meat, OR imitation crab meat	250 g

In a large skillet, heat butter over medium heat and sauté the onion and garlic until tender. Add the whole-kernel corn and chicken stock and bring to a boil. Reduce heat to low and simmer for 10 minutes. Stir in cereal cream, salt and pepper; simmer for 10 minutes. Meanwhile, in a small saucepan, over medium-high heat, cook potato, red pepper and celery in boiling water until tender, about 2 minutes. Stir the drained vegetables into the soup; add the cream-style corn and crab meat and heat through. Serve immediately, garnished with parsley or celery leaves.

Serves 4-6

Ham and White Bean Soup

A hearty and satisfying soup.

2 cups	dry white beans	500 mL
	cold water to soak and cook beans	
1 tbsp.	vegetable oil	15 mL
3	garlic cloves, minced	3
1	large onion, finely chopped	1
1 cup	chopped celery	250 mL
1 tsp.	dried thyme	5 mL
1 tbsp.	dried parsley	15 mL
½ tsp.	pepper	2 mL
6 drops	hot pepper sauce	6 drops
5 cups	chicken stock	1.25 L
2 cups	chopped ham	500 mL

Prepare beans as per instructions below. In a large saucepan, over medium heat, heat oil and sauté garlic, onion and celery until tender. Stir in remaining ingredients, including beans. Bring to a boil. Reduce heat and simmer gently for 10-15 minutes.

Serves 4

To Prepare Dried Beans:

- 1 cup (250 mL) dried beans yields about 2 cups (500 mL) cooked beans.
- To cook dried beans: rinse; sort and pick out the bad ones. Soak beans for 12 hours in 3 times their volume of cold water. Drain off water; rinse. In a saucepan, cover beans with 3 times their new volume of water and bring to a boil. Reduce heat and simmer, covered, for 1-2 hours, or until tender.
- For a quick soak, bring beans, with water to cover, to a boil; boil gently for 2 minutes. Remove from heat, cover and let stand for 1 hour. Drain off water; rinse. In a saucepan, cover beans with 3 times their new volume of water and bring to a boil. Reduce heat and simmer, covered, for 1-2 hours, or until tender.
- For added flavor, a ham bone may be added to the beans in the cooking process.

Sausage and Sauerkraut Soup

24-32 oz.	ham sausage, in ½" (1.3 cm) slices	680-907 g
3	medium potatoes, peeled, cubed	3
2	onions, chopped	2
3	garlic cloves, minced	2
2	carrots, in ¼" (1 cm) slices	2
1 cup	chopped celery	250 mL
6 cups	chicken stock	1.5 L
32 oz.	can sauerkraut, drained, rinsed	1 kg
28 oz.	can tomatoes, coarsely chopped	796 mL
¼ tsp.	dried sage	1 mL
½ tsp.	dried parsley	2 mL

In a large saucepan, combine sausage, potatoes, onions, garlic, carrots, celery and chicken stock; bring to a boil. Reduce heat; cover and simmer for 20 minutes, until potatoes are tender. Add remaining ingredients; mix well. Return to a boil. Reduce heat; cover and simmer 30 minutes longer. Serve immediately.

Serves 8-10

Tomato Tortellini Soup

A different way to serve tortellini – in a soup!

12½ oz.	pkg. tortellini, meat OR cheese filled	350 g
1	large onion, chopped	1
4	garlic cloves, minced	4
1 tbsp.	vegetable oil	15 mL
4 cups	beef stock	1 L
2 cups	water	500 mL
1 cup	chopped celery	250 mL
3	medium carrots, chopped	3
1 tsp.	EACH, dried basil, oregano	5 mL
⅛ tsp.	EACH, salt and pepper	0.5 mL
19 oz.	can tomatoes, coarsely chopped	540 mL
½ cup	tomato sauce	125 mL

Tomato Tortellini Soup *(continued)*

Cook tortellini according to package directions; drain and set aside. In a large saucepan, over medium heat, sauté onion and garlic in vegetable oil until tender. Add beef stock, water, celery, carrots and seasonings; cook over medium heat until vegetables are tender, approximately 10 minutes. Add tomatoes, tomato sauce and tortellini; cook for 10-15 minutes, or until heated through. Serve immediately. Top with Parmesan cheese, if desired.

Serves 6-8

Hamburger Soup

Served with fresh bread, this soup is a meal in itself.

1 tbsp.	vegetable oil	15 mL
1½ lbs.	lean ground beef	750 g
2	garlic cloves, minced	2
19 oz.	can tomatoes, broken	540 mL
10 oz.	can sliced mushrooms with liquid	284 mL
2 cups	beef stock	500 mL
3	medium carrots, chopped	3
1 cup	chopped celery	250 mL
2	medium potatoes, peeled, chopped	2
1 cup	frozen peas	250 mL
1	large onion, chopped	1
½ tsp.	EACH, dried parsley, thyme	2 mL
⅛ tsp.	EACH, salt and pepper	0.5 mL
14 oz.	can kidney beans	398 mL

In a large saucepan, over medium-high heat, heat oil and cook ground beef and garlic until all pink has gone. Drain off all fat; add tomatoes, mushrooms with liquid, beef stock, carrots, celery, potatoes, peas, onion, parsley, thyme, salt and pepper. Cover and simmer for 1 hour, stirring occasionally. Add kidney beans and simmer for 40-60 minutes, stirring occasionally. Serve immediately. Freezes well.

Serves 4-6

Vegetable Beef Barley Soup

A thick, chunky and flavorful soup.

1 lb.	beef stewing meat, cut into ½" (1.3 cm) cubes	500 g
2 tbsp.	vegetable oil	30 mL
2 cups	chopped onion	500 mL
2 cups	chopped celery	500 mL
4-6	garlic cloves, minced	4-6
4 cups	water	1 L
6 cups	beef stock	1.5 L
5	medium carrots, chopped	5
1 cup	pearl barley	250 mL
4 cups	sliced zucchini	1 L
¼ cup	chopped fresh parsley	60 mL
1 tsp.	dried thyme	5 mL
1 tsp.	dried basil	5 mL
½ tsp.	salt	2 mL
¼ tsp.	pepper	1 mL
14 oz.	can chick-peas (garbanzos), drained	398 mL
14 oz.	can kidney beans, drained	398 mL
19 oz.	can tomatoes	540 mL
	grated Parmesan cheese (optional)	

In a large saucepan, brown meat in oil. Add onion, celery and garlic. Cook until beef is no longer pink. Add water and stock; bring to a boil. Add carrots, barley, zucchini, parsley, thyme, basil, salt and pepper. Reduce heat; cover and simmer for 60 minutes, or until barley is tender. Add chick-peas, kidney beans and tomatoes. Simmer 20-30 minutes.

Serve immediately with fresh bread. Top individual bowls with Parmesan cheese, if desired.

Serves 12-15

Eggs

Baked

Soufflé

Quiches

Stratas

Baked Stuffed Eggs

This tasty, make-ahead, dish has always been a great hit with men.

8	hard-boiled eggs, shelled	8
1 tbsp.	sour cream	15 mL
4 tbsp.	mayonnaise	60 mL
2 tsp.	prepared mustard	10 mL
½ tsp.	salt	2 mL

Mushroom Cheese Sauce:

½ cup	chopped onion	125 mL
½ cup	chopped celery	125 mL
2 tbsp.	butter OR margarine	30 mL
10 oz.	can cream of mushroom soup	284 mL
1 cup	sour cream	250 mL
¾ cup	shredded Cheddar cheese	175 mL
½ tsp.	paprika	2 mL

Slice eggs in half lengthwise; remove yolks and set whites aside. In a bowl, mash yolks with a fork. Add sour cream, mayonnaise, mustard and salt. Mix well. Fill the egg whites; set aside. In a skillet, sauté onion and celery in butter until tender. Add soup and sour cream; mix well. Pour half the sauce into an ungreased 7 x 11" (18 x 28 cm) baking dish. Arrange stuffed eggs over the sauce. Spoon remaining sauce over eggs. Sprinkle with cheese and paprika. Cover and refrigerate overnight.

Preheat oven to 350°F (180°C). Remove eggs from refrigerator 30 minutes before baking. Bake, uncovered, for 25-30 minutes, or until heated through. Serve immediately.

Serves 6-8

Herbal Notes

- Use 3 times more fresh herbs than dried herbs to get the same flavor.
- When cooking with herbs, always "bruise" them first to release the oils that give them the flavor. (If fresh, cut , tear, or mash; if dry, crumble in hand and then add.)

Make-Ahead Scrambled Eggs

A creamy rich make-ahead breakfast dish for a busy weekend.

5 tbsp.	butter OR margarine, divided	75 mL
¼ cup	flour	60 mL
2 cups	milk	500 mL
2 cups	shredded sharp Cheddar cheese	500 mL
2 cups	sliced fresh mushrooms	500 mL
½ cup	finely chopped onion	125 mL
12	eggs, beaten	12
1 tsp.	salt	5 mL
10 oz.	pkg. frozen chopped broccoli, cooked, drained	283 g
1 cup	bread crumbs	250 mL

In a saucepan, melt 2 tbsp. (30 mL) butter. Add flour; cook and stir until the mixture begins to bubble. Gradually stir in milk; bring to a boil. Cook and stir for 2 minutes. Remove from heat. Stir in cheese until melted; set aside. In a large skillet, sauté mushrooms and onions in 2 tbsp. (30 mL) of butter until tender. Add eggs and salt; cook and stir until the eggs are completely set. Add the cheese sauce and broccoli. Pour into a well-greased 9 x 13" (23 x 33 cm) baking dish. Melt the remaining tablespoon (15 mL) of butter and toss with bread crumbs. Sprinkle over egg mixture. Cover and refrigerate overnight.

Preheat oven to 350°F (180°C). Remove eggs from refrigerator 30 minutes before baking. Bake, uncovered, for 30-45 minutes, or until top is golden brown.

Serves 6-8

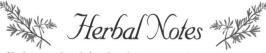

Herbal Notes

- Heat and sunlight are bad for herbs. Store them in a cool cupboard away from heat.
- Dried herbs lose most of their flavor after a year.
- Do not make more than one or two herbed dishes per meal.
- Do not wash fresh herbs until you are ready to use them. If they are wet, wrap in paper towel or dry at room temperature before storing them.

Make-Ahead Eggs Benedict

2	English muffins, split, toasted	2
8	thin slices of ham	8
4	eggs	4

Wine and Cheese Sauce:

2 tbsp.	butter OR margarine	30 mL
2 tbsp.	flour	30 mL
1 tsp.	paprika	5 mL
⅛ tsp.	EACH, salt and pepper	0.5 mL
1 cup	milk	250 mL
1 cup	shredded mozzarella cheese	250 mL
¼ cup	dry white wine	60 mL
4-5 drops	hot pepper sauce	4-5 drops
½ cup	fine bread crumbs OR cracker crumbs	125 mL
1 tbsp.	melted butter OR margarine	15 mL

In a well-greased 9" (23 cm) square baking dish, arrange split muffins, cut side up. Place 2 ham slices on each muffin half. Poach eggs in an egg poacher OR half fill a 10" (25 cm) skillet with water; bring just to boiling. Break 1 egg into a dish; carefully slide egg into water. Repeat with 3 more eggs. Simmer, uncovered, for 3 minutes, or just until set. Remove eggs with slotted spoon. Place 1 egg on top of each ham-topped muffin.

Sauce: In a medium saucepan, melt butter. Stir in flour, paprika, salt and pepper. Add milk all at once. Cook, stirring constantly until mixture is thickened and bubbly. Stir in cheese until melted. Stir in wine and hot pepper sauce. Remove from heat and carefully spoon sauce over muffin stacks. Cover; refrigerate overnight.

To serve: Preheat oven to 350°F (180°C). Remove eggs from refrigerator and uncover. Combine bread crumbs or cracker crumbs and 1 tbsp. (15 mL) of butter; sprinkle over muffin stacks. Place in oven and bake for 35-40 minutes, or until eggs are heated through. Serve immediately.

Serves 4

Pictured on page 51.

Eggs Benedict With a Twist

Hollandaise Sauce:

½ cup	butter	125 mL
2	egg yolks	2
1 tsp.	lemon juice	5 mL
⅓ cup	boiling water	75 mL
dash	EACH, salt, cayenne pepper	dash
8	slices bacon, cooked crisp	8
4	eggs	4
2	English muffins, split, toasted	2
2	medium tomatoes	2

Hollandaise Sauce: Divide butter into thirds. Beat egg yolks with lemon juice in top of double boiler; add ⅓ of the butter. Place over simmering, not boiling, water; cook, beating constantly, until butter melts and sauce starts to thicken; add the remaining butter, half at a time, the same way. Beat in boiling water slowly; continue cooking and stirring, still over simmering water, for 3 minutes, or until mixture thickens; remove from water. Stir in salt and cayenne pepper; cover sauce and keep warm in double boiler.

Grill bacon and reserve.

To poach eggs, use an egg poacher OR pour water into a large skillet to make a 2" (5 cm) depth; salt lightly; bring just to boil. Break eggs, 1 at a time into a cup, and slip into water. Simmer, basting often with water in skillet, about 3 minutes, or just until egg is set. Lift out with slotted spoon.

To Assemble: Place toasted muffin halves on plates. Top each with 2 bacon strips, 1 tomato slice and a poached egg. Top each with a generous serving of Hollandaise Sauce.

Serve immediately.

Serves 2

Basic French Omelet

Tasty basic omelet, just fill with your favorite filling.

3	eggs	3
2 tbsp.	water	30 mL
¼ tsp.	salt	1 mL
⅛ tsp.	pepper	0.5 mL
1 tbsp.	butter OR margarine	15 mL

Break eggs into a small bowl. Add the water, salt and pepper. Beat the eggs vigorously with a wire whisk or fork until the yolks and whites are mixed. In a 7" (18 cm) omelet pan or skillet, over medium heat, melt butter; tilt the pan so that the butter coats the entire surface of the pan. Pour in eggs all at once. Let eggs set around edge. Shake pan occasionally to keep omelet moving freely over the bottom of the pan. With spatula or egg turner, lift edge as it sets, tilting pan to allow uncooked egg mixture to run under omelet. Continue to shake pan for a few seconds longer, until you can feel the omelet sliding freely over the pan surface. When omelet is set but still moist on the surface, increase heat slightly to brown bottom. Remove pan from heat. Tilt pan away from you and, using the spatula or egg turner, lift the edge of the omelet and quickly fold in half. Slide omelet onto a plate and garnish as desired. Serve immediately.

Serves 1

Omelet Fillings:

When adding a filling to an omelet, prepare the filling and spread it over ½ of the cooked omelet with a spatula or spoon. Gently fold the other half over the filing and serve immediately.

Cooked Ham: In a small skillet over medium heat, melt 1 tbsp. (15 mL) of butter. Add ¾ cup (175 mL) of chopped, cooked ham; cook until hot; stir frequently to prevent burning.

Herbs: Add 4 tsp. (20 mL) mixed dried herbs or ¼ cup (60 mL) finely chopped fresh herbs to the beaten eggs before cooking. Parsley, chives and tarragon are suitable for omelets.

Omelet Fillings (continued):

Cheese: Sprinkle each omelet with ¼ cup (60 mL) of shredded Cheddar cheese or any mixture of cheeses just before folding omelet.

Creole Sauce: In a small skillet over medium heat, heat 1 tbsp. (15 mL) of vegetable oil. Add 6 tbsp. (90 mL) chopped green pepper, 6 tbsp. (90 mL) chopped celery and 2 tbsp. (30 mL) chopped onion; cook until tender, about 5 minutes, stirring occasionally. Add 2 medium tomatoes, peeled and chopped, ¼ tsp. (1 mL) dried oregano and ¼ tsp. (1 mL) salt. Mix well and simmer, covered, for 10 minutes, stirring often.

Eggs Florentine

An easy-to-make version of the very classic dish.

¼ cup	chopped onion	60 mL
1 tbsp.	butter OR margarine	15 mL
2 x 10 oz.	pkgs. frozen chopped spinach	2 x 283 g
8 oz.	cream cheese, cut into cubes	250 g
⅛ tsp.	EACH, salt and pepper	0.5 mL
6-8 drops	hot pepper sauce	6-8 drops
4	eggs	4
¼ cup	grated Parmesan cheese	60 mL

In large skillet, sauté onion in butter until tender but not brown. Add spinach, cream cheese, salt, pepper and hot pepper sauce. Cook over medium heat, separating spinach with a fork as it thaws. Stir to blend ingredients. With the back of a spoon, make 4 depressions in the spinach mixture, break an egg into each, being careful not to break the yolks. Cover skillet; cook until eggs are done as desired. Sprinkle with Parmesan cheese. Serve immediately.

Serves 4

Ham, Bacon and Cheese Bake

A delicious quick and easy brunch dish.

1 cup	diced, fully cooked ham	250 mL
¾ cup	shredded Swiss cheese	175 mL
6	slices bacon, cooked, crumbled	6
¾ cup	shredded, sharp Cheddar cheese	175 mL
3 tbsp.	chopped onion	45 mL
3 tbsp.	chopped green pepper	45 mL
1 cup	milk	250 mL
¼ cup	biscuit mix	60 mL
2	eggs	2
⅛ tsp.	EACH, salt and pepper	0.5 mL
8 drops	hot pepper sauce	8 drops

Preheat oven to 350°F (180°C). In a greased 10" (25 cm) quiche dish or pie plate, layer ham, Swiss cheese, bacon, Cheddar cheese, onion and green pepper. Place milk, biscuit mix, eggs, salt, pepper and hot sauce in a blender or food processor. Blend for 30-40 seconds. Pour over layers. Do not stir. Bake, uncovered, for 30-35 minutes, or until set and lightly browned. Let stand 5 minutes before cutting.

Serves 4-6

Morning Skillet

8	breakfast sausages	8
1 tbsp.	butter OR margarine	15 mL
1 cup	diced potatoes	250 mL
½ cup	chopped green onion	125 mL
½ cup	EACH, chopped green and red pepper	125 mL
1 cup	sliced fresh mushrooms	250 mL
6	eggs	6
¼ cup	milk	60 mL
⅛ tsp.	EACH, salt and pepper	0.5 mL
1 cup	shredded Cheddar cheese	250 mL

Morning Skillet *(continued)*

In a large skillet over medium heat, melt butter and cook sausages for 5-8 minutes, until nicely browned; remove from pan; cut into ½" (1.3 cm) pieces and set aside. In the drippings, stir-fry potatoes over medium heat until tender, about 10-12 minutes. Add onion, peppers and mushrooms; cook for 4-5 minutes, until tender-crisp. Stir in the sausage. In a large bowl, beat eggs, milk, salt and pepper; pour into skillet. Cook and stir gently until the eggs are set. Sprinkle with cheese and let stand until melted. Serve immediately with toast or biscuits.

Serves 4

Broccoli and Cheese Soufflé

2 cups	chopped broccoli florets	500 mL
¼ cup	butter OR margarine	60 mL
¼ cup	flour	60 mL
½ tsp.	dried thyme	2 mL
¼ tsp.	ground pepper	1 mL
1 cup	milk	250 mL
1-1½ cups	shredded Gouda cheese	250-375 mL
4	eggs, separated	4

In a small saucepan of boiling salted water, cook broccoli for 2 minutes, until tender-crisp. Drain; chill under cold running water. In a saucepan, melt butter over medium heat; add flour, thyme and pepper; cook; stir for 1-2 minutes. Gradually pour in milk; stirring constantly, cook for 5 minutes, until smooth and very thick. Remove from heat; stir in cheese until almost melted. Separate eggs. To the egg yolks, whisk in ½ cup (125 mL) of the cheese mixture; whisk back into the saucepan of cheese mixture. Fold in broccoli. Let cool completely. (Soufflé can be prepared to this point, covered and refrigerated for up to 12 hours. Cover and refrigerate egg whites; let come to room temperature.)

Preheat oven to 350°F (180°C). Beat egg whites until stiff peaks form; fold ¼ of whites into the broccoli-cheese mixture; fold in remaining whites. Spoon into a 3 x 7" (8 x 18 cm) soufflé dish. Bake for 1 hour, or until golden brown and tester inserted in center comes out clean.

Makes 4 servings

Mushroom and Cheese Strata

A simple cheesy make-ahead dish.

¼ cup	butter OR margarine	60 mL
3 cups	sliced fresh mushrooms	750 mL
½ cup	chopped onion	125 mL
½ cup	chopped celery	125 mL
½ cup	chopped green pepper	125 mL
½ tsp.	salt	2 mL
¼ tsp.	pepper	1 mL
½ cup	mayonnaise	125 mL
6	slices bread, crusts removed	6
2 tbsp.	butter OR margarine	30 mL
2	eggs, beaten	2
1½ cups	milk	375 mL
1 tbsp.	Worcestershire sauce	15 mL
½ tsp.	dry mustard	2 mL
1 cup	shredded Cheddar cheese	250 mL

In a large skillet over medium heat, melt ¼ cup (60 mL) of butter and sauté mushrooms, onion, celery and green peppers until soft. Sprinkle with salt and pepper. Remove from heat and let cool. Stir in mayonnaise. Spread bread with the soft butter and cut bread into ½" (1.3 cm) cubes. Place half of the bread cubes in a lightly buttered 9 x 13" (23 x 33 cm) baking dish. Pour sautéed vegetable mixture over. Add remaining bread cubes. In a large bowl, beat eggs; add milk, Worcestershire sauce and dry mustard and pour over casserole. Cover and refrigerate overnight. To bake, preheat oven to 325°F (160°C). Bake for 45 minutes. Remove from oven and sprinkle with cheese. Return to oven and continue baking for 15-25 minutes longer, or until knife inserted in the center comes out clean. Remove from oven and let set for 10 minutes. Cut into squares and serve.

Serves 6-8

Thanksgiving Day Brunch

Five-Fruit Breakfast Cocktail, page 156

Zesty Pumpkin Soup, page 83*

Weekender Quiche, page 109*

Peaches and Cream Breakfast, page 22

Marinated Vegetable Salad, page 64*

Carrot Pineapple Muffins, page 35

Plum Kuchen, page 40

Pictured recipes

Zesty Pumpkin Soup
Weekender Quiche
Marinated Vegetable Salad

Smoked Salmon Strata

Strata means layer in Italian; this delicious savory strata combines layers of whole-wheat bread, our famous west coast salmon and 2 different cheeses.

12	slices whole-wheat bread	12
½ lb.	smoked salmon, thinly sliced	250 g
2 cups	shredded Cheddar cheese	500 mL
2 cups	shredded mozzarella cheese	500 mL
3 cups	whole milk	750 mL
8	eggs	8
¼ cup	finely chopped fresh dillweed or 1 tsp. (5 mL) dried	60 mL
⅛ tsp.	freshly ground pepper sour cream (optional)	0.5 mL

Lightly butter a 9 x 13" (23 x 33 cm) baking dish. Snugly line the bottom of the dish with a single layer of sliced bread. If necessary, cut bread to fit pan so bottom of dish is completely covered. Arrange half the salmon on top of the bread. Sprinkle half the cheese over top. Cover with a second layer of bread. Cover with smoked salmon. Then sprinkle remaining cheese evenly over top. In a medium bowl, whisk milk with eggs, dillweed and pepper. Pour mixture evenly over entire surface. Cover the dish tightly with clear wrap and refrigerate overnight or for at least 8 hours.

Preheat oven to 350°F (180°C). Remove baking dish from refrigerator and bake, uncovered, for 45 minutes, or until edges are golden brown and center feels set when touched. Let cool for 10 minutes on a wire rack before serving. Sprinkle with a little fresh dillweed. Cut into squares. Serve with a dab of sour cream if you wish.

Serves 8-10

Bacon and Egg Pie

Scrambled eggs combined with a bacon and cheese sauce, and baked in a crust of garlic and cheese toast.

2 tbsp.	butter OR margarine, softened	30 mL
1	garlic clove, minced	1
8-9	slices French bread, cut ¼" (1 cm) thick	8-9
1 cup	shredded Cheddar cheese	250 mL
1¼ cups	milk	300 mL
4 tsp.	flour	20 mL
4 oz.	cream cheese	125 g
¼ tsp.	pepper	1 mL
⅛ tsp.	salt	0.5 mL
1 tbsp.	fresh dillweed	15 mL
8	eggs, beaten	8
2 tbsp.	milk	30 mL
¼ tsp.	salt	1 mL
2 tbsp.	margarine OR butter	30 mL
12	slices bacon, cooked crisp, crumbled	12
⅓ cup	sour cream	75 mL
1 cup	red OR green pepper, seeded, chopped (optional)	250 mL

Preheat oven to 400°F (200°C). In a small mixing bowl, stir together the 2 tbsp. (30 mL) softened butter and the garlic; spread on 1 side of each bread slice. Cut 5 slices of bread in half crosswise. Arrange remaining whole slices of bread, butter side up, on the bottom of a 12" (30 cm) pie plate or quiche pan, trimming as needed to cover the bottom. Arrange the half slices around the sides of the plate. Bake, uncovered, in oven about 8 minutes, or until the edges are crispy. Sprinkle with ½ cup (125 mL) of the shredded cheese; return to oven and bake about 1 minute more, or until cheese is melted. In a medium saucepan, stir together 1¼ cups (300 mL) milk and flour; stir in softened cream cheese, pepper and the first ⅛ tsp. (0.5 mL) of salt. Cook and stir until thickened and bubbly; cook and stir for 1 minute more. Stir in dillweed and set aside.

Bacon and Egg Pie *(continued)*

In a medium mixing bowl, beat together eggs, milk and the second ⅛ tsp. (0.5 mL) salt. In a large skillet melt 2 tbsp. (30 mL) butter over medium heat; pour in egg mixture. Cook, without stirring, until mixture begins to set on the bottom and around the edge. Using a large spoon or spatula, lift and fold partially cooked eggs so uncooked portion flows underneath. Continue cooking over medium heat until eggs are cooked throughout but are still glossy and moist. Fold in half of the cream cheese sauce and the bacon. Spoon egg mixture into crust; sprinkle with remaining shredded cheese. Bake at 350°F (180°C) for 10-15 minutes, or until heated through. Stir the sour cream into the remaining cheese sauce. If necessary, stir in a little milk to thin. Heat through; do not boil. Spoon sauce on top of pie and sprinkle with chopped peppers, if desired. Cut into wedges to serve.

Serves 6

Reuben Strata

1 tbsp.	Dijon mustard	15 mL
5-6	slices rye bread	5-6
¾ lb.	corned beef, thinly sliced	365 g
14 oz.	can sauerkraut, washed, well drained	398 mL
10 oz.	can tomato soup	284 mL
¼ cup	water	60 mL
¼ cup	finely chopped dill pickles	60 mL
1 cup	grated Swiss cheese	250 mL

Preheat oven to 350°F (180°C). Spread mustard on 1 side of each slice of bread. Arrange in a lightly buttered 9" (23 cm) square baking dish, filling in spaces with extra bread if necessary. Arrange corned beef evenly over bread. In a large bowl, combine sauerkraut, soup, water and dill pickles. Mix well and spread over corned beef. Bake for 20 minutes; top with cheese and bake for an additional 10-20 minutes. Serve immediately.

Serves 4-6

Spinach, Ham and Cheese Pie

Layers of spinach, ham and cheese make this an interesting and delicious dish.

1	onion, chopped	1
3	garlic cloves, minced	3
1 tbsp.	butter OR margarine	15 mL
2 x 10 oz.	pkgs. frozen spinach (thawed, drained)	2 x 283 g
	pastry for double-crust pie	
½ lb.	sliced ham	250 g
1 lb.	mozzarella cheese, sliced	500 g
2	sweet red peppers, cut into strips	2
7	eggs	7

Sauté onion and garlic in butter. Add spinach and cook until tender. Reserve ⅓ of pastry for top. Roll out remaining pastry to line a greased 9" (23 cm) springform pan or deep cake pan. Allow pastry to overhang. Layer half the ham, half the cheese, half the spinach mixture and half the red peppers. Beat 6 eggs and pour over this layer. Repeat layering with remaining ingredients. Roll out remaining pastry and cover. Seal edges; brush with remaining egg mixed with a bit of water. Cut vents in top. Bake at 400°F (200°C) for 45 minutes, or until golden. Serve warm or cold.

Makes 8-10 servings

Variation:

Instead of pastry, a hash brown crust may be used. Preheat oven to 425°F (220°C). Press 3 cups (750 mL) of frozen hash browns, thawed, into the bottom and up the sides of a 9" (23 cm) deep pie plate or cake pan. Drizzle with ⅓ cup (75 mL) of melted butter. Bake for 25 minutes. Remove from oven and add layers of filling as above. Top with additional ½ cup (125 mL) mozzarella cheese.

Weekender Quiche

A great make-ahead dish for a busy weekend – no crust means fewer calories and less work!

10	slices bacon	10
½ cup	chopped green pepper	125 mL
8	green onions, finely chopped	8
1 lb.	fresh mushrooms, sliced	500 g
3 tbsp.	chopped pimiento	45 mL
3 tbsp.	sherry	45 mL
12	eggs	12
1½ cups	milk	375 mL
1 tsp.	salt	5 mL
1 tsp.	dry mustard	5 mL
1 tsp.	dried thyme	5 mL
4 cups	grated Gruyère cheese	1 L

In a large skillet, over medium-high heat, fry bacon until crisp; remove from pan and chop or crumble. In the same pan, with 2 tbsp. (30 mL) of the drippings, over medium-low heat, sauté green pepper, onions and mushrooms until tender. Add pimiento and sherry. Cook until sherry evaporates, about 3 minutes. Remove from heat and set aside. In a large bowl, beat eggs and milk together until well blended; add salt, mustard and thyme and beat until well combined. Add bacon and mushroom mixture and 3 cups (750 mL) of grated cheese. Combine well and pour into a well-greased 9 x 13" (23 x 33 cm) baking pan or 2, 8" (20 cm) baking pans. Cover and refrigerate overnight. To bake preheat oven to 350°F (180°C). Uncover, place in oven and bake for 40 minutes. Remove from oven, sprinkle with the remaining 1 cup (250 mL) of cheese and continue to bake for 5 more minutes, or until cheese melts and a knife inserted in the center comes out clean. Remove from oven and let stand 20 minutes before cutting.

Serves 8

Pictured on page 103.

Smoked Salmon Quiche

	pastry for 9-10" (23-25 cm) quiche dish or pie plate	
1 tbsp.	butter OR margarine	15 mL
1 cup	sliced fresh mushrooms	250 mL
½ lb.	smoked salmon, chopped	250 g
1½ cups	grated Swiss cheese	375 mL
4	green onions, sliced	4
5	eggs	5
1 cup	milk	250 mL
½ cup	whipping cream	125 mL
½ cup	grated Parmesan cheese	125 mL
1½ tsp.	dried dillweed	7 mL
½ tsp.	salt	2 mL
¼ tsp.	pepper	1 mL

Preheat oven to 450°F (230°C). Line a 9-10" (23-25 cm) quiche pan or pie plate with pastry; prick surface with a fork and bake for 5 minutes. Remove from oven and cool slightly. In a skillet over medium-low heat, melt butter and sauté mushrooms for 5-8 minutes; set aside. Spread the chopped salmon evenly over the bottom of the pastry shell. Sprinkle with mushrooms, Swiss cheese and green onions. In a large bowl, with a wire whisk, beat eggs lightly; add milk, cream, Parmesan cheese, dillweed, salt and pepper. Blend well. Pour into pastry shell. Bake for 10 minutes; reduce heat to 350°F (180°C), and bake for an additional 15-20 minutes; or until center is almost firm, but still soft. Let stand for 10 minutes before serving. Garnish with fresh dillweed sprigs.

Serves 6-8

Savory Crab Cheesecake

Indulge guests with this rich, mild, cheesy, crab-flavored elegant cheesecake.

Crust:

¼ cup	melted butter OR margarine	60 mL
2 cups	crushed seasoned croûtons	500 mL
¼ cup	grated Parmesan cheese	60 mL
1 tsp.	garlic powder	5 mL

Cheesecake:

1 tbsp.	butter OR margarine	15 mL
1	medium onion, chopped	1
1½ cups	sliced fresh mushrooms	375 mL
3 x 8 oz.	cream cheese, softened	3 x 250 g
4	eggs	4
1½ cups	grated Cheddar cheese	375 mL
½ cup	mayonnaise	125 mL
2 tsp.	lemon juice	10 mL
8 drops	hot pepper sauce	8 drops
6 oz.	crab meat	170 g

Preheat oven to 350°F (180°C). In a small bowl, combine croûton crumbs with cheese and garlic powder; pour in melted butter and stir well to combine. Press into the bottom of a 9" (23 cm) springform pan and bake for 10 minutes. In a skillet over medium heat, melt butter and sauté onion and mushrooms until tender, about 3-5 minutes; set aside. Beat cream cheese; add 1 egg and beat until light. Beat in remaining eggs, 1 at a time, beating well after each addition. Add Cheddar cheese, mayonnaise, lemon juice and hot pepper sauce. Beat well to combine. Fold in crab meat, sautéed onion and mushrooms. Stir to combine well. Pour over crust in springform pan. Bake for 1-1½ hours. Center will quiver slightly when pan is shaken. Set on rack and run knife around top edge. Let set for 15-20 minutes; remove rim and cut into wedges to serve. Cheesecake may be served warm or cold. It can also be topped with sour cream or decorated as desired.

Serves 6-8

Ham and Shrimp Gâteau

6 tbsp.	butter OR margarine	90 mL
¼ cup	sliced green onion	60 mL
1 cup	sliced fresh mushrooms	250 mL
1 cup	diced cooked ham	250 mL
1 cup	tiny cooked shrimp	250 mL
3 tbsp.	flour	45 mL
1¼ cups	chicken stock	300 mL
¼ cup	whipping cream	60 mL
¼ tsp.	dry mustard	1 mL
¼ tsp.	salt	1 mL
¼ tsp.	pepper	1 mL
2 tbsp.	dry white wine	30 mL
1 cup	grated Parmesan cheese	250 mL
8	large crêpes	8

In a heavy skillet, over medium heat, melt 3 tbsp. (45 mL) of the butter and sauté green onions and mushrooms until tender. Add ham and shrimp. Stir in remaining butter until melted. Sprinkle with flour. Add chicken stock, cream, mustard, salt, pepper and wine. Cook until thick and bubbly. Add half of the cheese. Stir until melted. To assemble Gâteau, lightly butter a large 10-12" (25-30 cm) ovenproof shallow casserole or platter. Place a crêpe in the center, cover with a layer of the sauce. Repeat layers until all the sauce and crêpes have been used. Sprinkle top with remaining cheese. May be covered and refrigerated overnight at this point. To bake, preheat oven to 375°F (190°C). Bake for 40-50 minutes, or until Gâteau is piping hot and top is browned. Cut into wedges to serve.

Serves 4-6

Pictured on page 69.

Ham and Eggs Brunch Pizza

1	recipe of pizza dough*, page 116	1
2 tbsp.	butter OR margarine	30 mL
3	green onions, chopped	3
¼ cup	chopped green peppers	60 mL
1 cup	sliced fresh mushrooms	250 mL
8	eggs	8
¼ cup	milk	60 mL
⅛ tsp.	pepper	0.5 mL
2 cups	chopped cooked ham	500 mL
4 oz.	cream cheese, softened	125 g
1 cup	pineapple chunks	250 mL
1 cup	grated mozzarella cheese	250 mL

Prepare pizza dough as per instructions. Preheat oven to 425°F (220°C). Grease 12" (30 cm) pizza pan; roll out dough and line pan. Bake for 6-8 minutes, or until crust begins to brown. Remove from oven and set aside. In a large skillet, over medium heat, melt butter and add onions, pepper and mushrooms. Cook and stir until vegetables are tender, about 3-4 minutes. In a large bowl, beat eggs; add milk and pepper and beat well. Add egg mixture to vegetables in skillet and cook over medium heat 4-5 minutes, or until thoroughly cooked but still moist, stirring occasionally. Fold in ham; remove from heat. Spread cream cheese evenly over partially baked crust. Sprinkle the pineapple chunks over the cream cheese and spoon cooked egg mixture over top. Sprinkle with mozzarella. Bake 10-15 minutes, or until toppings are thoroughly heated and crust is golden brown. Remove from oven and garnish as desired. Serve immediately.

Serves 6-8

* For a very easy, very fast variation, use a prepared pizza crust.

Sausage and Egg Burritos

A taste of "Old Mexico" for brunch.

½ lb.	pork sausage, browned, drained, cut into ½" (1.3 cm) pieces	250 g
2 cups	frozen hash browns	500 mL
12	eggs	12
1	large onion, chopped	1
1	green pepper, seeded, chopped	1
1 cup	whole-kernel corn	250 mL
¼ tsp.	chili powder or more to taste	1 mL
12, 10"	flour tortillas, warmed	12, 25 cm
3 cups	shredded Cheddar cheese	750 mL
	salsa and sour cream (optional)	

Preheat oven to 350°F (180°C). In a large skillet, brown sausages; remove and set aside. Drain skillet and fry hash browns according to package directions; remove and set aside. In a large bowl, beat eggs; add onions, green pepper, corn and chili powder. Pour into the same skillet; over medium heat, cook and stir until eggs are set. Remove from heat. Add hash browns and browned sausage; mix gently. Place about ¾ cup (175 mL) of filling on each tortilla and top with about ¼ cup (60 mL) cheese. Roll up tortillas and place on a greased 9 x 13" (23 x 33 cm) baking dish. Bake for 20-30 minutes, or until heated through. Remove from oven and serve immediately with salsa and sour cream, if desired.

Serves 10-12

Herbal Mythology

Bay leaf from the Laurel tree is the herb most associated with nobility. From Greek mythology, a chief Greek god, Apollo, was in love with the beautiful Daphne, but she spurned his attentions. He asked her mother for help to keep her safe, so her mother turned her into a tree – the Laurel tree. Of course this was Apollo's favorite tree and he decreed that its leaves were to be bestowed on any who displayed extraordinary courage or excellence. This is the origin of the Greek tradition of crowning outstanding citizens, including Olympic athletes, with a wreath made of Laurel (bay) leaves.

Main Dishes

Pizza
Pastas
Savory Pies
Casseroles

Filled Pizza (Bread Machine)

For 1 lb. (500 g) bread machine – 1, 9" (23 cm) filled pizza or 1, 12" (30 cm) pizza crust. You can use any combination of filling you wish, this is our favorite.

Dough:

⅔ cup	water	150 mL
3 tbsp.	vegetable oil	45 mL
2 cups	flour	500 mL
3 tbsp.	sugar	45 mL
1 tsp.	salt	5 mL
¼ tsp.	freshly ground pepper	1 mL
1¼ tsp.	active dry yeast	6 mL

Filling:

1	egg	1
1 cup	ricotta cheese	250 mL
2 tbsp.	grated Parmesan cheese	30 mL
¼ tsp.	freshly ground pepper	1 mL
¼ lb.	Italian salami, sliced	125 g
½ cup	shredded mozzarella cheese	125 mL
½ cup	sliced red OR green peppers	125 mL

Add all ingredients for the dough in the order suggested by your bread machine manual. Process on the dough cycle according to the manufacturer's directions. At the end of the dough cycle, remove the dough from the machine and place on a floured surface. Preheat oven to 375°F (190°C). With a floured rolling pin, roll out the dough into a large circle no more than ¼" (1 cm) thick. Line a 9" (23 cm) pie plate with the dough, leaving at least a 4" (10 cm) overhang all around.

Filling: Beat the egg in a small bowl; add the ricotta cheese, Parmesan cheese and pepper. Stir to combine well. Spread one-third of the salami over the dough in the pie plate. Top with half of the ricotta mixture. Sprinkle on half of the mozzarella and peppers. Repeat the layers, ending with the last of the meat.

Filled Pizza *(continued)*

Pull the edges of the dough up over the filling. Pinch and press the edges of the dough together in the center to seal. Let the filled pizza rise for 15 minutes. Bake in preheated oven for 30-40 minutes. Baked pizza can be made up to a day in advance, refrigerated and reheated in oven.

Serves 4-6

Filled French Loaf

A satisfying and easy luncheon dish.

8 oz.	cream cheese, softened	250 g
10 oz.	frozen spinach (thawed, drained) finely chopped	283 g
1 cup	grated Cheddar cheese	250 mL
2 tsp.	dillweed	10 mL
1 cup	mayonnaise	250 mL
¼ cup	diced onion	60 mL
2	garlic cloves, crushed	2
12	strips bacon, crisply fried, crumbled	12
⅛ tsp.	EACH, salt and pepper	0.5 mL
1	French loaf	1

Preheat oven to 325°F (160°C). In a large bowl, beat cream cheese until smooth; add all other ingredients, except the French loaf, and fold together. Cut off end of loaf and hollow out loaf center. Fill with the cheese filling. Replace cut off end piece. Wrap with foil and bake for 1-1½ hours. Cool for 10 minutes then slice.

Serves 6-8

Variation:

 Crab-Filled French Loaf: Prepare as above, but use 4 oz. (113 g) can of crab meat instead of the bacon.

Springtime Spaghetti

A creamy, meatless dish for pasta lovers.

1 lb.	spaghetti OR very thin egg noodles, cooked according to package instructions	500 g
¼ cup	butter OR margarine	60 mL
4	garlic cloves, minced	4
2	large carrots, cut julienne	2
1	medium zucchini, cut julienne	1
1	small red OR green pepper, cut julienne	1
1 cup	whipping cream	250 mL
½ cup	grated Parmesan cheese	125 mL
¼ cup	chopped fresh dillweed or 1½ tbsp. (22 mL) dried	60 mL
½ tsp.	salt	2 mL
¼ tsp.	pepper	1 mL

Cook pasta according to package instructions; drain and set aside. In a large skillet, over medium heat, melt butter; add garlic and sauté for 1 minute. Add vegetables and cook over medium-high heat for 2 minutes, or until tender-crisp. Stir in cream, Parmesan cheese, dillweed, salt and pepper; combine well. Reduce heat to low and add pasta; toss gently to blend. Serve immediately with additional Parmesan cheese.
Serves 8

Bay Leaf

The bay leaf comes from the Laurel tree, known as Bay or Sweet Bay, which is an ever-green grown in the Mediterranean area. This leaf has a slightly wavy edge. The laurel tree is also grown in California. This leaf has a smooth edge and much less flavor.

The bay leaf releases its oil over a long period of time and therefore goes into the saucepan at the start of cooking. DO NOT CRUMBLE the bay leaf into the dish you are cooking as the leaves are very tough. Remove the leaves before serving.

Fresh Vegetable Pasta Sauce

For the pasta lovers who prefer a meatless tomato-based sauce.

2 tbsp.	vegetable oil	30 mL
1	medium onion, chopped	1
2	garlic cloves, minced	2
1½ cups	sliced fresh mushrooms	375 mL
6	tomatoes, chopped	6
1 tbsp.	dried basil	15 mL
1 tbsp.	dried oregano	15 mL
1 tbsp.	dried parsley	15 mL
2	bay leaves	2
2	carrots, shredded	2
1 cup	finely chopped celery	250 mL
1	medium zucchini, chopped	1
½ tsp.	salt	2 mL
¼ tsp.	pepper	1 mL
½ cup	tomato paste	125 mL

In a large skillet, over medium heat, heat oil and sauté onion, garlic and mushrooms until tender. Transfer to a large saucepan and add tomatoes, basil, oregano, parsley and bay leaves. Simmer over medium-low heat for 10-12 minutes, stirring occasionally. Add carrots, celery and zucchini; continue to cook until vegetables are tender soft, about 10-15 minutes. Remove bay leaves. Add salt, pepper and tomato paste and heat to boiling point. Serve immediately over your favorite pasta.

Serves 4-6

Bay Leaf

Bay leaf goes well in hearty soups, stews, pot roast and tomato-based spaghetti sauce. If you are poaching fish, put a leaf in the water; also, if roasting a chicken unstuffed, place several bay leaves in the cavity for a nice flavor. It is also one of the three ingredients of the classic "bouquet garni" of French cuisine.

Chicken and Pasta Thai Style

A taste of the Orient.

6 cups	any long, thin pasta, cooked according to package instructions	1.5 L
2 tbsp.	vegetable oil	30 mL
2 lbs.	boneless, skinless chicken breasts, in 1" (2.5 cm) strips	1 kg
1	onion, chopped	1
4	garlic cloves, minced	4
1	red pepper, cut julienne	1
1	green pepper, cut julienne	1
4 cups	chicken stock	1 L
2 tbsp.	liquid honey	30 mL
4 tbsp.	soy sauce	60 mL
1 tbsp.	rice vinegar	15 mL
½ cup	peanut butter	125 mL
3 tbsp.	cornstarch	45 mL
1½ tsp.	ground ginger	7 mL
¼ cup	sesame seeds, toasted	60 mL

Cook pasta according to package instructions; drain; set aside. In a large skillet, over medium-high heat, heat oil; sauté chicken until golden. Remove chicken; set aside and keep warm. In the same skillet, over medium-low heat, sauté onions and garlic until soft; add red and green peppers and continue to cook until tender-crisp, about 3 minutes. Remove from heat and set aside. In a clean skillet, combine chicken stock, honey, soy sauce and rice vinegar; whisk in peanut butter, cornstarch and ginger. Place over medium heat and cook, stirring constantly, until thickened and smooth. Add vegetables and reserved chicken; cook and stir until just bubbly and thickened. Spoon chicken mixture over pasta. Serve topped with sesame seeds.

Serves 6-8

Mexican Brunch

White Sangria, page 158

Chunky Corn Chowder, page 87*

Sausage and Egg Burritos, page 114

Shrimp and Pasta Bake, page 127

Shrimp and Vegetable Salad, page 68*

Eileen's Tea Biscuits – Spicy Cheddar Variation, page 32*

Mexican Wedding Cake, page 151

* Pictured recipes

  Chunky Corn Chowder
  Shrimp and Vegetable Salad
  Eileen's Tea Biscuits – Spicy Cheddar Variation

Savory Chicken and Spinach Cannelloni

6	cannelloni shells	6
2 tbsp.	butter OR margarine	30 mL
2	green onions, sliced	2
10 oz.	pkg. frozen, chopped spinach (thawed, well-drained)	283 g
1 cup	chopped cooked chicken	250 mL
1 cup	chopped cooked ham	250 mL
¼ cup	grated Parmesan cheese	60 mL
¼ cup	grated Romano cheese	60 mL
2	eggs, beaten	2
¾ tsp.	Italian seasoning	3 mL
¼ tsp.	ground pepper	1 mL

Cheese Sauce:

¼ cup	butter OR margarine	60 mL
3	garlic cloves, minced	3
¼ cup	flour	60 mL
1 tsp.	pepper	5 mL
2 cups	chicken stock	500 mL
2 cups	half-and-half cereal cream	500 mL
¼ cup	EACH, Parmesan and Romano cheese	60 mL

Preheat oven to 350°F (180°C). Parboil cannelloni shells according to package directions; drain; rinse in cold water and set aside. In a skillet, over medium-low heat, melt butter and sauté onions until tender; remove from heat and stir in remaining ingredients. Fill shells and place in a well-buttered 2-quart (2 L) baking dish. Set aside while sauce is prepared.

Sauce: In a skillet over medium-low heat, melt butter and sauté garlic for 2-3 minutes. Stir in flour and pepper; gradually add chicken stock and cream; stir constantly until mixture thickens. Reduce heat; add cheese and stir until cheese has melted.

Spoon sauce over filled cannelloni. Bake for 20-30 minutes, then broil for 5 minutes, or until sauce becomes golden and bubbles. Serve immediately.

Serves 3-4

Quick Creamy Turkey Fettuccine

½ lb.	fettuccine, cook according to package instructions	250 g
1 cup	broccoli florets	250 mL
1 cup	milk	250 mL
4 oz.	cream cheese, cubed	125 g
4	green onions, chopped	4
½ tsp.	Italian seasoning	2 mL
2	garlic cloves, minced	2
1 cup	cubed cooked turkey	250 mL
½ cup	Parmesan cheese, divided	125 mL

Cook pasta as directed on package. Add broccoli during the last 5 minutes of cooking; drain and set aside. In a medium saucepan, combine milk, cream cheese, onions, Italian seasoning and garlic. Cook over low heat until combined and smooth. Stir in turkey and ¼ cup (60 mL) of Parmesan cheese; heat through. Toss pasta and vegetables with sauce. Top with the remaining Parmesan cheese.

Serves 4

Spaghetti Carbonara

Wonderful with a green salad and fresh bread.

1 lb.	spaghetti, cook according to package instructions	500 g
1 lb.	bacon, diced	500 g
2 cups	sliced fresh mushrooms	500 mL
6	garlic cloves, minced	6
1	onion, finely chopped	1
¼ cup	olive oil	60 mL
3	eggs, lightly beaten	3
¼ cup	whipping cream	60 mL
½ tsp.	black pepper	2 mL
1 cup	grated Parmesan cheese	250 mL

Spaghetti Carbonara *(continued)*

Cook spaghetti; drain and set aside. In a skillet over medium heat, sauté the bacon, mushrooms, garlic and onions in the oil until tender. Drain oil. In a large bowl beat eggs lightly; whisk in cream; add pepper and Parmesan. Stir in bacon and mushroom mixture. Pour over spaghetti; toss well. Serve immediately.

Serves 6-8

Ham-Stuffed Manicotti

8	manicotti shells	8
½ cup	chopped onion	125 mL
3	garlic cloves, minced	3
1 tbsp.	vegetable oil	15 mL
3 cups	ground, fully cooked ham	750 mL
10 oz.	pkg. spinach, cooked, drained	283 g
10 oz.	can sliced mushrooms, drained	284 mL
3 tbsp.	grated Parmesan cheese	45 mL
1 cup	grated Swiss cheese, divided	250 mL
½ cup	chopped green pepper	125 mL
3 tbsp.	butter OR margarine	45 mL
3 tbsp.	flour	45 mL
2 cups	milk	500 mL
	paprika	
	chopped fresh parsley	

Cook manicotti as directed on package; set aside. In a large skillet, sauté onion and garlic in oil until tender. Remove from the heat. Add ham, spinach, mushrooms, Parmesan cheese and half of the Swiss cheese; set aside. In a saucepan, sauté green pepper in butter until tender. Stir in flour. Add milk; cook, stirring constantly until thickened and bubbly. Mix ¼ of the sauce into ham mixture. Stuff each manicotti shell with about ⅓ cup (75 mL) of filling. Place in a greased 9 x 13" (23 x 33 cm) baking dish. Top with remaining sauce; sprinkle with paprika. Cover and bake at 350°F (180°C) for 30 minutes, until heated through. Sprinkle with parsley and remaining Swiss cheese before serving.

Serves 8

Meat Sauce Lasagne

8	lasagne noodles	8
1 tbsp.	vegetable oil	15 mL
1	onion, chopped	1
3	garlic cloves, minced	3
1 lb.	lean ground beef	500 g
2 x 14 oz.	cans tomato sauce	2 x 398 mL
5½ oz.	can tomato paste	156 mL
10 oz.	can sliced mushrooms	284 mL
¾-1 cup	water	175-250 mL
1½ tsp.	oregano	7 mL
2	eggs, lightly beaten	2
2 cups	cottage cheese	500 mL
⅔ cup	grated Parmesan cheese	150 mL
4 tsp.	vegetable oil	20 mL
1 tsp.	salt	5 mL
8 oz.	mozzarella cheese, sliced	250 g

Cook lasagne according to package directions; set aside. In a large skillet, over medium heat, heat oil and sauté onion and garlic until tender. Add ground beef and brown. Remove excess fat and stir in tomato sauce, tomato paste, mushrooms with the liquid, water and oregano. Bring to a boil; reduce heat and let simmer for ½-¾ of an hour, adding more water if necessary. Remove from heat and set aside. In a bowl, beat eggs lightly and add cottage cheese, Parmesan cheese, oil and salt. Mix well to combine. To assemble, pour half of the meat sauce in the bottom of a 9 x 13" (23 x 33 cm) baking dish; top with half of the lasagne noodles; cover with the cottage cheese mixture; top with the remaining lasagne; pour the remaining meat sauce over top. Top with the cheese slices. Bake at 375°F (190°C) for 50-60 minutes.

Serves 8-10

Shrimp and Pasta Bake

This yummy savory dish is made up of layers of pasta, salsa and shrimp.

6-7 cups	cooked fusilli pasta	1.5-1.75 L
2	eggs, lightly beaten	2
1 cup	sour cream	250 mL
¾ cup	grated Parmesan cheese	175 mL
⅓ cup	ricotta cheese	75 mL
⅓ cup	chopped fresh parsley	75 mL
1 tsp.	dried basil	5 mL
1¾ cups	mild or hot salsa	425 mL
1 lb.	large shrimp, peeled, deveined, cooked, divided	500 g
2 cups	shredded mozzarella cheese, divided	500 mL

Cook pasta according to package instructions; drain and set aside. In a small bowl, combine eggs with sour cream. Stir in Parmesan and ricotta cheeses, parsley and basil; set aside. Place half of the pasta in a well-greased 9 x 13" (23 x 33 cm) baking dish; top with salsa and half the shrimp; half the mozzarella cheese and the remaining pasta. Spread the egg mixture over pasta; top with remaining shrimp and mozzarella cheese. Place in oven and bake at 350°F (180°C) for 20-30 minutes. Let stand 8-10 minutes before serving.

Serves 6-8

Thyme

This strong-flavored herb, one of the oldest recorded culinary herbs, comes in many varieties. The one we are most familiar with is called garden or common thyme. It enhances the flavor of beef – sprinkle over beef roast before cooking; use in meat loaf, hamburgers, spaghetti sauce, hearty beef soups or stews. It has a special affinity for fish dishes – chowders, seafood salads and baked fish. Use in stuffings for chicken and turkey. A wonderful enhancer for almost all vegetables. Thyme also blends well with the flavors of garlic, basil and lemon. Because it is actually a member of the mint family, thyme even sparks up fruit desserts like applesauce, rhubarb and berry compotes and cobblers. An easy-to-grow plant because it requires no special care, thyme dries and freezes well.

Lobster Pasta Sauce

2-3 cups	cooked fine egg noodles	500-750 mL
2 tbsp.	butter OR margarine	30 mL
1	small onion, chopped	1
½ cup	sliced fresh mushrooms	125 mL
1 tbsp.	chopped fresh parsley or 1 tsp. (5 mL) dried	15 mL
2 tbsp.	flour	30 mL
1½ cups	hot milk	375 mL
1 cup	shredded sharp Cheddar cheese	250 mL
4 oz.	can lobster, well drained	113 g
	salt and pepper (optional)	

Cook pasta according to package instructions. In a large skillet, over medium heat, melt butter; add onions, mushrooms and parsley. Cook for 3-4 minutes. Reduce heat to low and stir in flour; cook for 2 minutes. Slowly add milk; continue stirring and cooking over very low heat for 8-10 minutes. Stir in cheese. Add lobster, salt and pepper if desired; mix well and cook for 2-5 minutes over very low heat. Spoon over hot cooked pasta or toast points.

Serves 4

Shrimp and Snow Peas with Pasta

4 cups	rotini pasta, cooked	1 L
¼ cup	flour	60 mL
1 cup	mayonnaise	250 mL
2½ cups	milk	625 mL
½ cup	white wine	125 mL
1¼ cups	grated Parmesan cheese	300 mL
3 cups	cooked medium shrimp	750 mL
2 cups	snow peas	500 mL
3 cups	sliced fresh mushrooms	750 mL
	grated Parmesan cheese	

Shrimp and Snow Peas with Pasta *(continued)*

Cook pasta according to package instructions. In a saucepan, combine flour and mayonnaise; place over medium heat and whisk in milk. Cook, stirring constantly, for 6-8 minutes, or until sauce is thickened. Stir in wine and Parmesan cheese. Stir in shrimp, snow peas, cooked pasta and mushrooms. Place in a greased 3-quart (3 L) casserole. Sprinkle with additional Parmesan cheese. Bake at 375°F (190°C) for 45-60 minutes, or until lightly browned.

Serves 6-8

Creamy Seafood Pasta

A creamy dill sauce loaded with seafood over a bed of pasta.

2 tbsp.	flour	30 mL
2 cups	sour cream	500 mL
3 cups	shredded Monterey Jack cheese	750 mL
2 tbsp.	butter OR margarine	30 mL
8 oz.	crab meat	250 g
⅛ tsp.	pepper	0.5 mL
1 lb.	scallops, fresh or frozen	500 g
1 lb.	medium shrimp, cooked	500 g
3 tbsp.	fresh dillweed	45 mL
1 lb.	angel hair pasta	500 g
	parsley for garnish	

In a saucepan, whisk together flour and sour cream. Stir in cheese and butter. Place over medium-low heat and bring to a boil. Cook, stirring constantly, for 2 minutes. Remove from heat and add crab meat and pepper; set aside and keep warm. Place scallops in a small saucepan with a small amount of water; cook over medium heat for 5-7 minutes. Drain scallops and add to the crab mixture. Add shrimp and dill and place over medium-low heat until heated through. Cook pasta according to package directions; drain and top with the hot seafood mixture. Garnish with parsley and serve immediately.

Serves 6-8

Salmon Cannelloni

12	cannelloni shells	12

Salmon Filling:

15½ oz.	can pink salmon, drained and flaked	440 g
½ cup	sour cream	125 mL
2	green onions, chopped	2
1 tsp.	grated lemon rind	5 mL
¼ tsp.	salt	1 mL

Creamed Dill Sauce:

3 tbsp.	butter OR margarine	45 mL
3 tbsp.	flour	45 mL
1½ cups	milk	375 mL
1 tsp.	dried dillweed	5 mL
½ tsp.	salt	2 mL
2 tbsp.	lemon juice	30 mL
1 cup	shredded Swiss cheese	250 mL

Prepare cannelloni according to package instructions; drain.

Filling: Combine all filling ingredients; mix well. Carefully spoon into cannelloni shells and set aside.

Sauce: In a saucepan over medium heat, melt butter; stir in flour. Slowly whisk in milk. Add dillweed and salt and cook, stirring constantly, until mixture is bubbling and smooth. Remove from heat and stir in lemon juice. Pour a thin layer of sauce on bottom of a well-greased 9 x 13" (23 x 33 cm) baking dish. Place stuffed cannelloni in baking dish in a single layer. Cover with remaining sauce. Sprinkle with cheese. Cover dish and bake at 350°F (180°C) for for 35-40 minutes. Remove cover; place under broiler for 2-3 minutes, or until lightly browned.

Serves 6

Crab and Rice Casserole

Layers of crab and rice with a mushroom, cheese, yogurt sauce. Delightful!

1 cup	uncooked rice	250 mL
2 x 6 oz.	cans crab meat	2 x 170 g
2 tbsp.	butter OR margarine	30 mL
½ cup	sliced celery	125 mL
½ cup	chopped green pepper	125 mL
¼ cup	chopped onion	60 mL
10 oz.	can cream of mushroom soup	284 mL
1 cup	shredded Cheddar cheese	250 mL
1 cup	plain yogurt	250 mL
¼ cup	chopped pimiento	60 mL
⅛ tsp.	Worcestershire sauce	0.5 mL
½ tsp.	salt	2 mL

Cook rice according to package directions; set aside. Drain crab meat; flake and set aside. In a large skillet, over medium heat, melt butter and sauté the celery, green pepper and onion until tender, about 3-5 minutes. Remove from heat and stir in mushroom soup, cheese, yogurt, pimiento, Worcestershire sauce and salt. Layer rice and crab meat in a greased 9 x 13" (23 x 33 cm) baking dish; pour sauce over. Bake at 350°F (180°C) for 30 minutes.

Serves 6-8

Floral Meanings

Acacia – I want to be your friend
Almond Blossom – Encouragement, you can do it
Apple Blossom – You are preferred
Aster – You are always happy
Begonia – I can depend on you
Bluebell – You are gentle and faithful
Buttercup – You home is important to you

Turkey Pot Pie

1 cup	sliced carrots	250 mL
½ cup	sliced celery	125 mL
1 cup	cooked peas	250 mL
3 cups	cubed, cooked turkey	750 mL
1	medium onion, sliced	1
3 tbsp.	butter OR margarine	45 mL
3 tbsp.	flour	45 mL
1 tsp.	salt	5 mL
⅛ tsp.	pepper	0.5 mL
½ tsp.	dried savory	2 mL
1 cup	half-and-half cereal cream	250 mL
1 cup	chicken stock	250 mL
	pastry for 2-crust pie	

In a saucepan, over medium-high heat, combine carrots and celery; cook until tender; drain and combine with the peas and turkey. In a skillet over medium heat, sauté onion in butter until translucent and tender. Stir flour and seasonings into the onion mixture; gradually add cream and chicken stock; cook, stirring constantly, until thickened. Combine with the turkey and vegetables and set aside.

Preheat oven to 425°F (220°C). Roll out pastry on a lightly floured surface. Line a 9" (23 cm) pie plate or a 1½-quart (1.5 L) casserole with pastry dough. Pour filling into pie shell. Roll out second crust and top pie. Trim; crimp to seal and cut slits in top. Bake 12-15 minutes; reduce temperature to 350°F (180°C) and bake for additional 45-50 minutes.

Makes 1 pie

Floral Meanings

Carnation (white) – Purity
Carnation (deep red) – I have a broken heart
Chrysanthemum – I will always hope
Clematis – Poor but honest
Clover (white) – Think of me

Shane's Turkey Ragoût

This recipe comes from our dear nephew Shane Campbell, a forester who also enjoys cooking and eating.

4 lbs.	turkey thighs	1.8 kg
2 tbsp.	flour	30 mL
1¼ tsp.	salt	6 mL
½ tsp.	pepper	2 mL
2 tbsp.	vegetable oil	30 mL
1	large onion, chopped	1
2	garlic cloves, minced	2
½ tsp.	dried sage	2 mL
¼ tsp.	fennel seed	1 mL
2 cups	chicken stock	500 mL
19 oz.	can crushed tomatoes	540 mL
2	fennel bulbs, sliced	2
3	sweet potatoes OR yams, cut into 1" (2.5 cm) cubes	3

Rinse turkey, remove skin and cut into 1" (2.5 cm) pieces. In a large bowl, combine flour, ½ tsp. (2 mL) salt and ¼ tsp. (1 mL) pepper; add the turkey pieces and coat well. In a large saucepan or Dutch oven, over medium heat, heat the oil and fry the turkey pieces just until browned. Add the onion, garlic, ¾ tsp. (3 mL) salt, ¼ tsp. (1 mL) pepper, sage, fennel seed and ½ cup (125 mL) chicken stock. Cook until onion is tender and add remaining chicken stock, tomatoes, fennel and sweet potatoes. Bring to a boil; reduce heat and simmer until vegetables are tender, approximately 1 hour. Ragoût may also be cooked in a crock pot. After browning the turkey pieces, transfer them to the crock pot; add all other ingredients and cook on low heat for 6-8 hours.

Serves 4-6

Cheddar Ham and Asparagus

1 lb.	fresh or frozen asparagus, cut into 1" (2.5 cm) pieces	500 g
1 tbsp.	cornstarch	15 mL
1½ cups	milk, divided	375 mL
2 tbsp.	butter OR margarine	30 mL
1 tsp.	salt	5 mL
½ tsp.	pepper	2 mL
½ tsp.	dried parsley flakes	2 mL
1½ lbs.	fully cooked ham, cubed	750 g
3	hard-cooked eggs, chopped	3
2 cups	shredded Cheddar cheese	500 mL

In a saucepan, cook asparagus in a small amount of water until tender; drain and set aside. In a saucepan, mix cornstarch and 2 tbsp. (30 mL) milk. Set over medium-low heat and add butter, salt, pepper and remaining milk. Cook, stirring constantly, until mixture thickens and bubbles. Add parsley, ham, eggs, cheese and asparagus; cook and stir over low heat until ham is warmed and cheese is melted. Serve over toast points or biscuits.

Serves 4-6

Floral Meanings

Clover (red) – You are sweet
Columbine – Bound to win
Crocus – Always happy
Daffodil – You are welcome
Dahlia – Graciousness
Daisy – Innocence
Fern – Sincerity

Ham and Corn Croquettes

3 cups	chopped cooked ham	750 mL
1 cup	cream-style corn	250 mL
1	small onion, chopped	1
2	eggs, lightly beaten	2
2 tbsp.	minced fresh parsley	30 mL
½ tsp.	ground pepper	2 mL
¾ cup	dry bread crumbs, divided	175 mL
2 tbsp.	cornmeal	30 mL
3 tbsp.	vegetable oil	45 mL
2	green peppers, seeded, cut into thin strips	2
¼ tsp.	salt	1 mL

Tarragon Mustard Sauce:

¼ cup	sour cream	60 mL
¼ cup	mayonnaise	60 mL
1 tsp.	dried tarragon	5 mL
½ tsp.	Dijon mustard	2 mL

In a large bowl, combine ham, cream-style corn, onion, egg, parsley, pepper and ½ cup (125 mL) of bread crumbs. Mix well to combine and form into 6 patties. Mix remaining bread crumbs with cornmeal; coat patties with crumb mixture and set aside. Heat 1 tbsp. (15 mL) oil in skillet over medium heat; add peppers and salt and cook until softened, about 5 minutes. Remove from pan and keep warm. Add the remaining 2 tbsp. (30 mL) of oil to skillet; heat over medium heat. Add ham patties and cook until browned, approximately 4 minutes per side. Reduce heat to low; cook until heated through, approximately 8-10 minutes.

Sauce: In a small bowl mix together sour cream, mayonnaise, tarragon and mustard.

On a serving plate arrange patties and peppers and top with sauce.

Serves 4-6

Dilly Ham Balls

1 lb.	fully cooked ham, ground	500 g
½ cup	dry bread crumbs	125 mL
¼ cup	finely chopped green onions	60 mL
1 tsp.	dried dillweed	5 mL
¼ cup	milk	60 mL
1	egg, lightly beaten	1
1 tsp.	Dijon mustard	5 mL
¼ tsp.	pepper	1 mL
4 tbsp.	vegetable oil	60 mL
	noodles for 6	

Creamy Dill Sauce:

2 tbsp.	flour	30 mL
1 cup	water	250 mL
1 cup	sour cream	250 mL
2 tsp.	dried dillweed	10 mL
¼ tsp.	pepper	1 mL
	cooked noodles for 6	

In a large bowl, combine ground ham, bread crumbs, onions, 1 tsp. (5 mL) dillweed, milk, egg, mustard and ¼ tsp. (1 mL) pepper. Mix well to combine. Shape into 1" (2.5 cm) balls. In a large skillet over medium heat, heat oil and cook ham balls until nicely browned, approximately 5 minutes. Remove ham balls to a serving dish; cover and keep warm.

Sauce: In the skillet, over medium-low heat, blend flour with the ham drippings. Gradually add water and stir until smooth. Cook, stirring constantly, until mixture thickens. Add sour cream, dillweed and pepper; heat through, but do not allow to boil. Pour over ham balls. Serve over cooked noodles.

Serves 6

Sweets

Fresh Fruit

Cheesecakes

Baked Fruit

Tortes

Cakes

Pineapple Orange Fruit Dip

½ cup	pineapple juice	125 mL
¼ cup	sugar	60 mL
1 tbsp.	cornstarch	15 mL
1 tbsp.	orange juice	15 mL
2 tsp.	grated orange rind	10 mL
1	egg, lightly beaten	1
4 oz.	cream cheese, softened	125 g
	assortment of fresh fruit	

In a small saucepan, combine pineapple juice, sugar, cornstarch, orange juice and orange rind. Place over medium heat and cook, stirring constantly, for 5 minutes, or until clear and thickened. Slowly stir some hot mixture into the beaten egg. Return all to saucepan and cook over low heat until mixture thickens slightly. Cool for 5 minutes. Whisk in cream cheese until smooth. Refrigerate 2 hours, or until very cold. Serve dip in a dish surrounded by fresh fruit.

Makes 1½ cups (375 mL)

Caramel Fruit Dip

8 oz.	cream cheese, softened	250 g
¾ cup	brown sugar	175 mL
1 cup	sour cream	250 mL
2 tsp.	vanilla	10 mL
1 cup	cold milk	250 mL
3½ oz.	pkg. vanilla instant pudding mix	100 g
	assorted fresh fruit	

In a large bowl, beat cream cheese and brown sugar until smooth. Add sour cream, vanilla, milk and pudding mix, beating well after each addition. Cover and chill for at least 1 hour.

Makes 3½ cups (875 mL)

Christmas Morning Brunch

Spicy Cranberry Warmer, page 160*

Baked Fruit and Wine, page 153*

Make-Ahead Scrambled Eggs, page 95

Ham and Corn Croquettes, page 135

Salad Supreme, page 59

Overnight Oven French Toast, page 23

Cinnamon Marzipan Coffeecake, page 50*

Amaretto Fruit Bread, page 47

Spiced Pumpkin Apple Muffins, page 37*

* Pictured recipes

Spicy Cranberry Warmer
Baked Fruit and Wine
Cinnamon Marzipan Coffeecake
Spiced Pumpkin Apple Muffins

Decorative Sugared Fresh Fruit

Use to decorate a fresh fruit platter, a cheese tray or a special cake.

1 cup	red grapes	250 mL
1 cup	green grapes	250 mL
¼ cup	whole cranberries, fresh or frozen	60 mL
¾ cup	pecan halves	175 mL
6	small prune plums	6
½ cup	sugar	125 mL
2 tbsp.	marshmallow cream	30 mL
4 tsp.	warm water	20 mL

Cut grapes into small bunches of 3 or 4 grapes each. Place sugar in a large shallow bowl. Spread out sheets of waxed paper for coated fruit. Combine marshmallow cream and water in a small bowl. Brush grapes, cranberries, pecans and plums lightly with marshmallow cream mixture. Spoon sugar onto fruit and nuts until evenly coated. Place on waxed paper to air-dry. Prepare 4-6 hours ahead of the time needed.

Chocolate-Dipped Strawberries

32	medium-large strawberries with stems	32
1½ cups	semisweet chocolate chips	375 mL
1½ tsp.	vegetable oil	7 mL
	icing (confectioner's) sugar (optional)	

Rinse strawberries and pat dry. Line 2 baking sheets with waxed paper. Place chocolate chips and oil in double boiler; place over hot water. Stir continuously until chocolate is melted and smooth. Hold strawberries at stem end and dip in melted chocolate to cover two-thirds of each berry. Allow excess chocolate to drip off; place berries on waxed paper to cool. Let harden. If desired, icing sugar may be sifted over finished berries.

Strawberry Fancies

An easy, colorful and delicious presentation.

24	large fresh strawberries	24
1 cup	whipping cream, whipped	250 mL
¼ cup	icing (confectioner's) sugar	60 mL
1 tbsp.	amaretto	15 mL

Wash strawberries, remove stems to form a flat base and allow to dry. With a sharp knife, slice each strawberry in half vertically to within ¼" (1 cm) of base. Cut each half into 3 wedges to form 6 petals. Be careful not to slice through base. Pull petals apart slightly. In a small bowl, whip cream; add icing sugar and amaretto. With a small spoon or pastry bag fill each strawberry with the cream mixture.

Makes 24 strawberries

Fruit Dessert Bowl

20	large marshmallows	20
2 cups	whipping cream, divided	500 mL
¼ cup	icing (confectioner's) sugar	60 mL
1 tsp.	vanilla	5 mL
19 oz.	can crushed pineapple, well drained	540 mL
1 cup	halved green grapes	250 mL
1 cup	flaked coconut	250 mL
1	pound cake OR angel food cake, cubed	1
6	large oranges, peeled, sectioned	6
¼ cup	toasted slivered almonds	60 mL

Place marshmallows and ¼ cup (60 mL) of whipping cream in the top of a double boiler; heat over boiling water until marshmallows are melted and mixture is smooth. Cool completely. Whip the remaining cream until thick; add icing sugar. Fold into marshmallow mixture. Fold in vanilla, drained pineapple, grapes and coconut. Place half of the cake cubes in the bottom of a 3-quart (3 L) clear glass bowl. Top with half of the orange sections. Top with half of the cream mixture. Repeat layers. Sprinkle with almonds. Chill until serving time.

Serves 10-12

Jellied Fruit Salad

3 oz.	pkg. lemon gelatin powder	85 g
3 oz.	pkg. orange gelatin powder	85 g
2 cups	boiling water	500 mL
1 cup	cold water	250 mL
1	lemon, juice of	1
10 oz.	can crushed pineapple, drained, juice reserved	284 mL
2	bananas, sliced	2
10 oz.	can mandarin orange segments, drained	284 mL
2-3 cups	miniature marshmallows	500-750 mL

Pineapple Cheese Topping:

1 cup	pineapple juice, reserved from pineapple	250 mL
½ cup	sugar	125 mL
2 tbsp.	flour	30 mL
1	egg, well-beaten	1
2 cups	whipping cream, whipped	500 mL
½ cup	grated Cheddar cheese	125 mL

In a large bowl, combine gelatin powders and boiling water. Stir to dissolve completely, then add the cold water. Set in refrigerator until syrupy. Remove gelatin and add the juice of 1 lemon, drained crushed pineapple, bananas, oranges and miniature marshmallows. Return to refrigerator until set completely, or overnight.

Topping: In a saucepan, combine the reserved pineapple juice (adding water to make 1 cup [250 mL] if necessary), sugar, flour and egg. Cook, stirring constantly, over medium-low heat until mixture thickens. Cool, then put in refrigerator to chill. In a separate bowl, beat whipping cream until soft peaks form. Fold into the cooled egg mixture and pour over gelatin mixture. Sprinkle with grated cheese.

Serves 8-10

Creamy Raspberry Tiramisu

Cream, raspberries, chocolate – a classic combination for a sophisticated treat.

2 x 10 oz.	pkgs. frozen unsweetened raspberries	2 x 283 g
3	egg yolks	3
½ cup	sugar	125 mL
⅓ cup	brandy OR raspberry liqueur	75 mL
2 cups	mascarpone cheese*	500 mL
1½ cups	whipping cream	375 mL
24	small, soft ladyfingers, halved	24
2 tbsp.	brandy OR raspberry liqueur	30 mL
¼ cup	icing (confectioner's) sugar	60 mL
3 x 1 oz.	squares white chocolate, chopped or shaved	3 x 30 g

In a colander, thaw raspberries (set aside a few for decoration); reserve juice; set aside. In large bowl, beat egg yolks with sugar until light. Beat in ⅓ cup (75 mL) of liqueur. Cook gently in a double boiler over simmering water. Stir constantly, until thickened. Custard mixture should be thick and creamy. Remove from heat and cool. Beat mascarpone cheese until smooth and then slowly beat in cooled custard. Whip 1 cup (250 mL) cream until stiff; gently fold into the cheese mixture. Set aside. Line bottom of an 8-cup (2 L) glass bowl with 12 ladyfinger halves. Combine 3 tbsp. (45 mL) reserved raspberry juice and 2 tbsp. (30 mL) of brandy or raspberry liqueur and brush over the ladyfingers. Spread with ¼ of the mascarpone mixture. Sprinkle ⅓ of the chopped or shaved chocolate over top. Sprinkle with ⅓ of the raspberries. Repeat twice. Layer with remaining 12 ladyfinger halves; brush with juice mixture and top with remaining mascarpone mixture. Cover lightly and refrigerate for at least 4 hours or overnight. Whip remaining ½ cup (125 mL) of cream; add icing sugar and mound over tiramisu. Garnish with chopped or shaved chocolate and raspberries.

Makes 8-10 servings

* If mascarpone is not available, substitute ½ cup (125 mL) sour cream and 2 tbsp. (30 mL) butter beaten into 16 oz. (500 g) softened cream cheese.

Fresh Strawberry Cheesecake

Coconut Vanilla Wafer Crust:

1 cup	vanilla wafer crumbs	250 mL
½ cup	angel flaked coconut	125 mL
⅓ cup	melted butter OR margarine	75 mL

Strawberry Cream Cheese Filling:

4 cups	hulled fresh strawberries	1 L
3 x 8 oz.	cream cheese, softened	3 x 250 g
1 cup	sugar	250 mL
½ cup	orange juice	125 mL
1 tbsp.	lemon juice	15 mL
2 tbsp.	unflavored gelatin (2, 7 g env.)	30 mL
½ cup	cold water	125 mL
1 cup	whipping cream, whipped	250 mL
½ cup	whipping cream, whipped	125 mL
	several reserved strawberries	

Crust: Grease sides only of a 9" (23 cm) springform pan. Line with a strip of waxed paper wide enough to reach top of pan. Combine crumbs, coconut and butter and press onto bottom of pan.

Filling: Reserve several strawberries for garnish. Cut 2, ¼" (1 cm) slices from center part of enough strawberries to press a single row of slices around base edge of pan. Slice remaining strawberries to make 2 cups (500 mL). Blend or mash prepared strawberries. In a large bowl, beat softened cream cheese, sugar, orange juice and lemon juice. Soften gelatin in cold water; stir over low heat until dissolved. Beat into cheese mixture. Refrigerate until mixture just begins to set. Fold in whipped cream and pour into prepared pan. Refrigerate several hours or overnight. Remove cake from pan. Remove waxed paper and garnish cake with whipped cream and strawberry slices.

Makes 12-14 servings

Pineapple Cheesecake

This no-bake recipe is our mother's favorite dessert. A soothing conclusion to any meal.

1⅓ cups	graham crumbs	325 mL
¼ cup	butter OR margarine, melted	60 mL
2 tbsp.	sugar	30 mL
5 oz.	pkg. lemon pie filling	140 g
½ cup	sugar	125 mL
2	eggs, separated	2
½ cup	pineapple juice	125 mL
1½ cups	water	375 mL
1 cup	drained crushed pineapple	250 mL
8 oz.	cream cheese	250 g

Combine crumbs, butter and 2 tbsp. (30 mL) sugar. Set aside ¼ of the crumb mixture and press the remainder into a 9 x 13" (23 x 33 cm) pan. In a large saucepan, combine the pie filling, ¼ cup (60 mL) of sugar, egg yolks, pineapple juice, water and crushed pineapple. Cook over medium-low heat until mixture boils and thickens. Remove from heat; add the cream cheese and beat until well blended. Beat the egg whites and add the ¼ cup (60 mL) of sugar; beat until stiff. Fold into the lemon mixture. Blend well and pour over crumb mixture in pan. Sprinkle the remaining crumbs on top. Chill 6-8 hours or overnight.

Serves 12-15

Floral Meanings

Forget-Me-Not – Please don't forget me
Geranium – Warm regards
Heather – I am lonely
Holly – We will rejoice together
Honeysuckle – Devotion
Iris – Have faith in me
Ivy – I cling to you

Chocolate Sour Cream Cheesecake

A creamy, chocolate delight.

⅓ cup	butter OR margarine	75 mL
2 tbsp.	sugar	30 mL
1½ cups	graham crumbs	375 mL
2 x 8 oz.	cream cheese, softened	2 x 250 g
1¼ cups	sugar	300 mL
⅓ cup	cocoa powder	75 mL
1 tsp.	vanilla	5 mL
2	eggs	2
1 cup	sour cream	250 mL
2 tbsp.	sugar	30 mL
½ tsp.	vanilla	2 mL
½ cup	whipping cream, whipped	125 mL
1 tbsp.	shaved semisweet chocolate	15 mL

Melt butter in a small saucepan; stir in 2 tbsp. (30 mL) of sugar and crumbs. Press crumb mixture on bottom and 1½-2" (4-5 cm) up sides of an 8" (20 cm) springform pan; refrigerate. Beat cream cheese in medium bowl with electric mixer until smooth; add 1¼ cups (300 mL) sugar and cocoa; then 1 tsp. (5 mL) vanilla and the eggs, beating until smooth. Pour into prepared crust. Bake at 375°F (190°C) for 25 minutes. Remove cake but do not turn off oven. Combine sour cream, 2 tbsp. (30 mL) sugar and ½ tsp. (2 mL) vanilla in a small bowl; spread over baked filling. Return cake to oven; bake 10 minutes. Cool on wire rack. Chill thoroughly before serving. Remove pan rim. Garnish cheesecake with whipped cream and shaved chocolate.

Serves 12-15

Apple and Cinnamon Torte

Delicious apple and cinnamon flavors on a shortbread base.

Shortbread Base:

½ cup	butter, softened	125 mL
⅓ cup	sugar	75 mL
1 cup	flour	250 mL
⅓ cup	raspberry OR apricot jam	75 mL

Cream Cheese Filling:

8 oz.	cream cheese, softened	250 g
¼ cup	sugar	60 mL
1	egg	1
1 tsp.	vanilla	5 mL

Apple Cinnamon Topping:

3 cups	peeled, cored, thinly sliced apples	750 mL
½ cup	sugar	125 mL
2 tsp.	ground cinnamon	10 mL
¾ cup	sliced almonds	175 mL

Base: Preheat oven to 450°F (230°C). In a bowl, cream butter and sugar together thoroughly. Blend in flour. Press evenly onto bottom and 1½" (4 cm) up sides of a 9" (23 cm) springform pan. Spread jam evenly over bottom of crust.

Filling: In a large bowl, beat together the cream cheese, sugar, egg and vanilla with an electric mixer until smooth and light. Spread over jam.

Topping: Toss apples, sugar and cinnamon together to coat well. Spoon over filling. Sprinkle with almonds. Bake for 10 minutes, then reduce heat to 400°F (200°C) and bake for additional 25-30 minutes, or until set and apples are tender. Cool slightly, then remove pan rim. Serve slightly warm or at room temperature.

Serves 8

Triple Almond Torte

This recipe comes from dear Italian friends who bake it on special holidays.

1 cup	sugar	250 mL
8 oz.	almond paste	250 g
¼ cup	butter, at room temperature	60 mL
4	eggs	4
2 tbsp.	amaretto	30 mL
1 cup	flour	250 mL
1 tsp.	baking powder	5 mL
4 oz.	mascarpone cheese*	250 g
2 tbsp.	amaretto	30 mL
½ cup	whipping cream, whipped	125 mL
	shaved chocolate	
	toasted sliced almonds	

Preheat oven to 325°F (160°C). In a large bowl, beat sugar, almond paste and butter with an electric mixer on low speed until blended. Beat in eggs and amaretto until smooth and well combined. Combine flour and baking powder; sprinkle over egg mixture and beat just until combined. Pour batter into a well-greased and floured 9" (23 cm) springform pan. Bake for 50-60 minutes, or until cake tester inserted in the center comes out clean. Remove from oven, cool in pan for 10 minutes. Loosen pan rim and cool cake completely on a wire rack. When cake is completely cool, remove pan rim.

Just before serving, beat mascarpone cheese; add amaretto and beat well to combine. Whip cream until soft peaks form; fold in mascarpone mixture. Transfer cake to serving plate; mound whipped cream mixture on top of cake. Top with shaved chocolate and toasted almonds.

Serves 10-12

 * See mascarpone note on page 144.

Dream Cake

Delicate orange-flavored cake, decorated with sugared roses for a Mother's Day Brunch or Bridal Shower Brunch.

⅔ cup	butter OR margarine	150 mL
1⅓ cups	sugar	325 mL
⅔ cup	fresh orange juice	150 mL
3 tbsp.	fresh lemon juice	45 mL
1 tsp.	grated orange peel	5 mL
1 tsp.	grated lemon peel	5 mL
2	eggs	2
2 cups	cake flour	500 mL
2 tsp.	baking powder	10 mL
1 tsp.	salt	5 mL

Coconut Orange Frosting:

1 cup	flaked coconut	250 mL
¼ cup	sugar	60 mL
2 tbsp.	fresh orange juice	30 mL
1 tbsp.	fresh lemon juice	15 mL
4 tsp.	grated orange peel, divided	20 mL
1 cup	whipping cream, whipped	250 mL

Preheat oven to 375°F (190°C). In a large mixing bowl, cream butter and sugar. Add juices and peel; mix well (mixture may appear curdled). Add eggs, 1 at a time, beating well after each addition. Sift flour with baking powder and salt; add to creamed mixture and mix well. Pour into 2 greased and floured 8" (20 cm) cake pans. Bake 25-30 minutes, or until cake tester inserted into middle of cake comes out clean. Cool cake in pans for 10 minutes before removing cakes to a wire rack to cool completely.

Frosting: Combine coconut, sugar, juices and peel; mix well. Let stand for 10-15 minutes, or until sugar is dissolved. Fold in whipped cream. Spread between cake layers and over the top. Decorate with sugared roses or/and edible flowers.

Serves 10-12

Sugared Roses:

Ensure roses are clean and dry. Have a variety to work with; leave some roses whole, separate some into petals and have some buds. Whisk 1 egg white lightly. Use a small paintbrush and brush egg white onto all surfaces. Sprinkle with a light coating of granulated sugar. Place candied flowers on waxed paper and dry at room temperature for a minimum of 24 hours, or until thoroughly dry. These may be stored in a tightly covered cardboard container.

Mexican Wedding Cake

Very moist, rich and delicious

2 cups	flour	500 mL
2 cups	sugar	500 mL
1 tsp.	baking soda	5 mL
2	eggs, well beaten	2
1 cup	chopped walnuts	250 mL
14 oz.	can crushed pineapple and juice	398 mL

Cream Cheese Topping:

8 oz.	cream cheese	250 g
¼ cup	butter OR margarine	60 mL
2 cups	icing (confectioner's) sugar	500 mL
1 tsp.	vanilla	5 mL

Preheat oven to 350°F (180°C). Beat eggs, add all other ingredients. Pour into a 9 x 13" (23 x 33 cm) greased pan. Bake for 30-40 minutes.

Cream Cheese Topping: While cake is baking, combine all topping ingredients in a double boiler; place over water and cook until smooth, stirring constantly. Pour over hot cake as soon as it comes out of the oven.

Serves 15-20

Pictured on the back cover.

Mom's Baked Apple Dumplings

A cinnamon-flavored apple, wrapped in a sweet biscuit dough and baked in a butterscotch syrup. A delightful treat.

Butterscotch Syrup:

2 cups	brown sugar	500 mL
3 cups	hot water	750 mL
¼ cup	butter OR margarine	60 mL
1 tsp.	vanilla	5 mL
2 cups	flour	500 mL
4 tsp.	baking powder	20 mL
2 tbsp.	sugar	30 mL
½ tsp.	salt	2 mL
2 tbsp.	butter OR margarine	30 mL
⅞ cup	milk	205 mL
6	apples, peeled, cored, quartered	6
2 tbsp.	sugar	30 mL
½ tsp.	ground cinnamon	2 mL

For Syrup: In a large saucepan, combine sugar and water, place over medium heat and bring to a boil; reduce heat to low; add butter and continue cooking for 5 minutes, or until sugar is totally dissolved. Remove from heat; add vanilla. Stir well and set aside.

For Dumplings: In a large bowl combine flour, baking powder, sugar and salt. Mix well to combine. With pastry blender or 2 knives, cut in butter until crumbly. Add milk, mixing with a fork until soft dough is formed. Transfer dough to a floured surface and roll to a 12 x 18" (30 x 45 cm) rectangle. Cut into 6 equal squares. Place a peeled, cored apple in the center of each square. Combine the sugar and cinnamon in a small bowl and sprinkle evenly over apples. Moisten edges of dough with milk and bring together, covering the apple completely. Pinch to seal well. Reheat syrup on medium heat just to the boiling point.

Mom's Baked Apple Dumplings *(continued)*

Carefully space the dumplings in a 9 x 13" (23 x 33 cm) pan; pour over boiling syrup. Place dumplings in oven and bake at 425°F (220°C) for 10 minutes; reduce heat to 350°F (180°C) and bake for additional 35-40 minutes, or until fruit is soft and dumplings are golden brown. Serve warm with ice cream or whipped cream.

Variation:

 Whole peaches or pears may be used in place of apples.

Baked Fruit and Wine

12 oz.	can frozen orange juice concentrate (thawed)	340 g
2 tbsp.	cornstarch	30 mL
4 cups	peeled, cored, sliced apples	1 L
19 oz.	can pineapple chunks, with juice	540 mL
19 oz.	can pitted cherries, with juice	540 mL
1½ cups	fresh or frozen cranberries	375 mL
6 oz.	pkg. dried apricots, cooked, drained	175 g
1 cup	cooked, drained figs	250 mL
1 cup	cooked, drained prunes	250 mL
¼ cup	white wine (optional)	60 mL

Preheat oven to 350°F (180°C). In a large bowl combine orange juice concentrate and cornstarch; stir until smooth. Add all fruit; stir to coat. Pour mixture into a buttered 3-quart (3 L) casserole. If desired, pour wine over all. Cover and bake for 50-60 minutes, or until hot and bubbly. Serve immediately with a dollop of sweetened whipped cream.

Serves 12

Pictured on page 139.

Fast Fudge Cake

A fast, easy recipe to make for your chocolate fix.

19 oz.	pkg. dark chocolate cake mix, 2-layer size	520 g
3½ oz.	instant chocolate pudding mix	100 g
1 cup	sour cream	250 mL
½ cup	vegetable oil	125 mL
4	eggs	4
2 tbsp.	amaretto	30 mL
½ tsp.	almond extract	2 mL
2 cups	semisweet chocolate chips	500 mL

Chocolate Amaretto Glaze:

4 x 1 oz.	squares semisweet chocolate	4 x 30 g
3 tbsp.	butter OR margarine	45 mL
2 tbsp.	amaretto	30 mL
1 tsp.	vegetable oil	5 mL

Preheat oven to 350°F (180°C). Lightly grease and flour a 10" (25 cm) bundt pan. Combine cake mix, pudding mix, sour cream, oil, eggs, amaretto and almond extract in a large bowl. Beat with electric mixer at medium speed for 2 minutes. Stir in chocolate chips. Pour into prepared pan. Bake for 55-60 minutes, or until toothpick inserted in center comes out clean. Cool in pan for 10 minutes. Remove from pan; invert onto wire rack. Cool cake then top with the following glaze.

Glaze: Over low heat, melt together the chocolate and butter in a small saucepan. Stir in the amaretto and oil. Spoon glaze over the cooled cake. If you wish, you may garnish with sliced almonds, sugared fruit or edible flowers.

Makes 1 cake

Drinks

Breakfast

Spirited Coolers

Chilled & Hot Punches & Teas

Frosted Coffees

Hot Chocolate

Morning Orange Drink

Nutritious and delicious.

12½ oz.	frozen orange juice concentrate (thawed)	355 mL
2 cups	cold water	500 mL
2 cups	milk	500 mL
⅔ cup	sugar	150 mL
2 tsp.	vanilla extract	10 mL
20	ice cubes	20

Combine the thawed orange juice concentrate, water, milk, sugar and vanilla in a blender and process at high speed. Add the ice cubes, a few at a time, blending until smooth. Serve immediately.

Serves 8-12

Pictured on page 51.

Five-Fruit Breakfast Cocktail

8 cups	cranberry juice	2 L
4 cups	apple juice	1 L
12½ oz.	can frozen pineapple juice concentrate, undiluted	355 mL
12½ oz.	can frozen orange juice concentrate, undiluted	355 mL
12½ oz.	can frozen lemonade concentrate, undiluted	355 mL
3	whole cloves	3
4	cinnamon sticks	4
4 cups	water (optional)	1 L

In a large saucepan or Dutch oven, combine juices, lemonade, cloves and cinnamon sticks. Bring to a boil. Reduce heat; cover and simmer for 1 hour. Add water if desired. Serve hot or cold.

Makes 16, 6-oz. (170 mL) servings

Teaberry Sangria

¾ cup	sugar	175 mL
3 cups	water	750 mL
2	oranges, sliced	2
1	lemon, sliced	1
6	teabags	6
10 oz.	pkg. frozen sliced strawberries in syrup (slightly thawed), undrained	283 g
10 oz.	pkg. frozen raspberries in syrup (slightly thawed), undrained	283 g
3 cups	ice water	750 mL
2 cups	lemon-lime carbonated beverage, chilled	500 mL

In a medium saucepan over medium-high heat, combine sugar and 3 cups (750 mL) of water. Stir constantly until sugar is dissolved. Bring to a boil. Add orange and lemon slices and boil 1 minute. Remove from heat; add teabags. Cover and let stand 5 minutes. Remove teabags and let tea mixture cool. When ready to serve, pour into pitcher; add undrained strawberries and raspberries, ice water and lemon-lime beverage.

Makes 10, 7-oz. (189 mL) servings

Variation:

 For a spirited **Red Wine Sangria**, substitute 3 cups (750 mL) red wine for the 3 cups (750 mL) of ice water.

Floral Meanings

Lavender – Sweets to the sweet
Lilac – Unadorned beauty
Lily – Austere purity
Lily of the Valley – Doubly dear
Marigold – Honesty
Nasturtium – Optimism

White Sangria

Great for a summer brunch.

2 x 26 oz.	bottles dry white wine	2 x 750 mL
½ cup	orange-flavored liqueur	125 mL
½ cup	sugar	125 mL
2	EACH, lemons, limes, oranges, thinly sliced	2
¾ cup	halved green grapes	175 mL
3 cups	club soda	750 mL

Combine wine, liqueur and sugar in a pitcher or bowl. Stir until sugar is dissolved. Add sliced lemons, limes, oranges and green grapes. Refrigerate for at least 1 hour. Just before serving, add soda and stir gently. Serve over ice.

Serves 8-10, 8-oz. (250 mL) glasses

Pictured on the back cover.

Creamy Champagne Raspberry Punch

Raspberries, champagne and ice cream – all in a glass.

10 oz.	pkg. frozen raspberries in syrup (thawed)	283 g
¼ cup	sugar	60 mL
3¼ cups	dry white champagne OR sparkling white grape juice, chilled	770 mL
2 cups	vanilla ice cream, softened	500 mL

In blender or food processor, purée raspberries with syrup and sugar until smooth; strain to remove seeds. In a large pitcher or punch bowl, combine raspberry purée, champagne or grape juice and softened ice cream; stir until frothy and well blended. Serve immediately in frosted champagne glasses or punch cups.

Makes 8, 6-oz. (170 mL) servings

Hot Orange and Pineapple Punch

A wonderful warming drink to serve on any occasion.

6 cups	unsweetened pineapple juice	1.5 L
2 cups	unsweetened orange juice	500 mL
½ cup	sugar	125 mL
¼ cup	lemon juice	60 mL
¼ tsp.	ground nutmeg	1 mL
3¼ cups	dry white wine	770 mL
	cinnamon sticks	
	fresh pineapple wedges	

In a large saucepan, combine pineapple juice, orange juice, sugar, lemon juice and nutmeg. Bring to a boil, stirring until sugar dissolves. Reduce heat and stir in wine. Heat through but do not boil. Pour into heat-proof glasses or mugs. Garnish each serving with a cinnamon stick stirrer and pineapple wedge.

Makes 12, 8-oz. (250 mL) cups

Floral Meanings

Orange Blossom – Happiness in marriage
Pansy – I'm thinking about you
Petunia – I believe in you
Poppy – Forgetfulness
Rose (Red) – I love you
Rose (White) – Worthy of love
Rosemary – Remembrance

Spicy Cranberry Warmer

3	whole cloves	3
2	cinnamon sticks	2
2	whole allspice	2
4 cups	apple juice	1 L
⅓ cup	brown sugar	75 mL
4 cups	cranberry juice	1 L
	additional cinnamon sticks for garnish (optional)	

Place whole cloves, cinnamon sticks and whole allspice in a double thickness of cheesecloth. Bring up corners of cloth and tie with a string, or if desired, place loose spices in saucepan and strain before serving. Pour apple juice into a large saucepan with the spices. Set on medium-low heat; cover and simmer for 5 minutes. Stir in sugar and simmer for 5 minutes longer. Add cranberry juice and heat to simmering temperature. Serve hot in mugs. Garnish with cinnamon sticks if desired.

Serves 8-10

Pictured on page 139.

Hot Mulled Tea

A nice hot drink for your winter brunch.

4 cups	boiling water	1 L
6	teabags	6
½ cup	sugar	125 mL
1	orange, cut into slices	1
4	whole cloves	4
4	cinnamon sticks	4
½ tsp	ground nutmeg	2 mL
1½ cups	cranberry cocktail	375 mL

Hot Mulled Tea *(continued)*

In a heatproof container, pour the boiling water over teabags, sugar, orange slices and all spices. Stir to dissolve sugar. Cover and let stand for 5 minutes. Heat cranberry drink; combine with tea mixture. Remove tea bags and serve piping hot.

Makes 6, 7-oz. (189 mL) servings

Hot Spiced Tea

A nice hot spiced beverage to serve for a cold winter's day brunch.

12 cups	water	3 L
5-6	whole cloves	5-6
3	cinnamon sticks	3
5	tea bags	5
3 cups	orange juice	750 mL
1 cup	lemon juice	250 mL
1 cup	sugar	250 mL
1	whole lemon, thinly sliced	1
1	whole orange, thinly sliced	1

Combine water, cloves and cinnamon in a large saucepan. Boil. Add tea bags. Cover saucepan; remove from heat and steep for 5 minutes. Remove tea bags. In a medium saucepan, heat orange juice, lemon juice and sugar over medium heat. Stir until sugar dissolves. Pour into spiced tea. Add lemon and orange slices. Keep hot but do not boil.

Makes 25, 6-oz. (170 mL) servings

Creamy Frosted Coffee

Quick, easy and good to the last drop.

1 cup	cold whipping cream	250 mL
¼ cup	icing (confectioner's) sugar	60 mL
1 cup	strong cold coffee	250 mL
4	scoops vanilla ice cream	4

Beat whipping cream until soft peaks form; add icing sugar and beat until stiff. Divide coffee evenly among 4 tall glasses. Divide whipped cream among the glasses, making sure it touches the glass all around. Top with a scoop of ice cream.

Serves 4

Chilly Café au Lait

2 tsp.	instant coffee	10 mL
¼ cup	boiling water	60 mL
2 tbsp.	sugar	30 mL
2 cups	cold milk	500 mL

Combine coffee, boiling water and sugar until dissolved. Cool completely and stir in cold milk. Serve immediately.

Makes 2 cups (500 mL)

Frozen Hot Chocolate

Rich, Smooth and Delicious

⅓ cup	cocoa powder	75 mL
2 x 1 oz.	squares semisweet chocolate	2 x 30 g
⅔ cup	whipping cream, divided	150 mL
½ cup	sugar	125 mL
1 tbsp.	butter OR margarine	15 mL
2 cups	milk	500 mL

In a large saucepan, over low heat, combine cocoa powder, chocolate, ¼ cup (60 mL) of the whipping cream, sugar and butter. Stir constantly until chocolate and butter are melted and sugar is dissolved. Gradually whisk in milk and another ¼ cup (60 mL) of cream. Bring just to a boil. Pour into a 9" (23 cm) square cake pan. Let stand for 15 minutes. Cover and freeze for at least 12 hours. Remove from freezer; let stand at room temperature for 5 minutes. Break into small pieces. Transfer to food processor along with the 2 tbsp. (30 mL) whipping cream. Purée until mixture is thick, smooth and creamy. Spoon into 4 goblets and serve immediately.

Serves 4

Floral Meanings

Snowdrop – Pure goodness
Sweet Pea – I long for you
Sweet William – Pleasant dreams
Tulip – Unrequited love
Violet – Modesty
White Heather – Good luck

Menu Suggestions

Easter Brunch

Teaberry Sangria, page 157
Creamy Frosted Coffee, page 162
Champagne Fruit Cups, page 56
Make-Ahead Eggs Benedict, page 96
Shrimp and Snow Peas with Pasta, page 128
Parmesan Vegetable Toss, page 64
Jo's Hot Cross Buns, page 54
Apple Cinnamon Muffins, page 34
Pineapple Cheesecake, page 146

Bridal Shower Brunch

White Sangria, page 158
Chilled Raspberry Soup, page 78
Savory Crab Cheesecake, page 111
Strawberry and Cheese Salad, page 60
Layered Chicken Salad, page 67
Eileen's Tea Biscuits, page 32
Herbed Scones, page 31
Dream Cake, page 150
Strawberry Fancies, page 142
Chocolate-Dipped Strawberries, page 141

Mother's Day Brunch

Morning Orange Drink, page 156
Creamy Blueberry Soup, page 78
French Toast Deluxe, page 21
Make-Ahead Eggs Benedict, page 96
Poppy Seed and Lemon Muffins, page 36
Fast Fudge Cake, page 154

Father's Day Brunch

Chilly Café au Lait, page 162
Frozen Hot Chocolate, page 163
Symphony of Fresh Fruits, page 57
Pancakes with Bacon, page 12
Baked Stuffed Eggs, page 94
Grilled Sausages
Oatmeal Muffins, page 38
Chocolate Sour Cream Cheesecake, page 147

Canada Day Brunch

Five-Fruit Breakfast Cocktail, page 156
Dill Pickle Soup, page 79
Smoked Salmon Strata, page 105
Ham and Shrimp Gâteau, page 112
Broccoli Bacon Salad, page 63
English Tea Scones, page 28
Welsh Cakes, page 27
Fresh Strawberry Cheesecake, page 145

Thanksgiving Day Brunch

Five-Fruit Breakfast Cocktail, page 156
Zesty Pumpkin Soup, page 83
Weekender Quiche, page 109
Peaches and Cream Breakfast, page 22
Marinated Vegetable Salad, page 64
Carrot Pineapple Muffins, page 35
Plum Kuchen, page 40

Grey Cup Party Brunch

Sausage and Sauerkraut Soup, page 90
Crab and Rice Casserole, page 131
Meat Sauce Lasagne, page 126
Italian Salad, page 66
Herbed Scones, page 31
Eileen's Tea Biscuits, page 32
Creamy Raspberry Tiramisu, page 144

Mexican Brunch

White Sangria, page 158
Chunky Corn Chowder, page 87
Sausage and Egg Burritos, page 114
Shrimp and Pasta Bake, page 127
Shrimp and Vegetable Salad, page 68
Mexican Wedding Cake, page 151

Christmas Morning Brunch

Spicy Cranberry Warmer, page 160
Baked Fruit and Wine, page 153
Make-Ahead Scrambled Eggs, page 95
Ham and Corn Croquettes, page 135
Salad Supreme, page 59
Overnight Oven French Toast, page 23
Cinnamon Marzipan Coffeecake, page 50
Amaretto Fruit Bread, page 47
Spiced Pumpkin Apple Muffins, page 37

Index

Share A Taste of Brunch

Order A Taste of Brunch at $14.95 per book plus $3.00 (total order) for postage and handling.

A Taste of Brunch – number of books _____ x $14.95 = $ ____
A Taste of Christmas – number of books _____ x $14.95 = $ ____
Shipping and handling charge _____ = $ 3.00
Subtotal _____ = $ ____
In Canada add 7% GST OR 15% HST where applicable _____ = $ ____
Total enclosed _____ = $ ____

U.S. and international orders payable in U.S. funds / Price is subject to change.

NAME: _____
STREET: _____
CITY: _____ PROV./STATE _____
COUNTRY _____ POSTAL CODE/ZIP _____

Please make cheque or money order payable to:
Three Sisters Publishing Inc.
12234 – 49 Street
Edmonton, Alberta, Canada   T5W 3A8
www.3sistersbooks.com

For fund raising or volume purchase prices, contact
Three Sisters Publishing. Please allow 3-4 weeks for delivery.

Share A Taste of Brunch

Order A Taste of Brunch at $14.95 per book plus $3.00 (total order) for postage and handling.

A Taste of Brunch – number of books _____ x $14.95 = $ ____
A Taste of Christmas – number of books _____ x $14.95 = $ ____
Shipping and handling charge _____ = $ 3.00
Subtotal _____ = $ ____
In Canada add 7% GST OR 15% HST where applicable _____ = $ ____
Total enclosed _____ = $ ____

U.S. and international orders payable in U.S. funds / Price is subject to change.

NAME: _____
STREET: _____
CITY: _____ PROV./STATE _____
COUNTRY _____ POSTAL CODE/ZIP _____

Please make cheque or money order payable to:
Three Sisters Publishing Inc.
12234 – 49 Street
Edmonton, Alberta, Canada   T5W 3A8
www.3sistersbooks.com

For fund raising or volume purchase prices, contact
Three Sisters Publishing Inc.
Please allow 3-4 weeks for delivery.

A Taste of Christmas

A Treasury of Holiday Recipes, Menus, Customs, Crafts and Gift-Giving Ideas

by Jacquie Schmit ❦ Eileen Mandryk ❦ Jo Wuth

The special magic of Christmas includes the tantalizing aromas of Christmas baking and heartwarming gifts of homemade delicacies. Tempting recipes use everyday ingredients and make-ahead suggestions for easy preparation. Menu ideas for the whole holiday season range from Cookie Exchanges to Holiday Open House parties to Christmas and New Year's Eve buffets, Christmas and New Year's Day dinners plus festive brunch, après skating or skiing and appetizer party ideas. Numerous ethnic recipes and Christmas customs from many parts of the world will enrich your own Christmas traditions and enhance your enjoyment of the holidays

Retail $14.95
172 pages
ISBN 1-895292-85-9

6" x 9"
6 full-color food photos
perfect bound